ROMANCE YOUR BRAND

BUILDING A MARKETABLE GENRE FICTION SERIES

ZOE YORK

Request · Read · Return

...Your Library. Delivered.

This item was purchased for the Library through Zip Books, a statewide project of the NorthNet Library System, funded by the California State Library.

ZoYo Press

London, Ontario, CANADA

www.ZoeYork.com

www.romanceyourbrand.com

In memory of my beloved Baba, once a two-year-old migrant child, and for everyone who actively works to make this world a better place for children.

Borders are bullshit and all human beings should have a right to live free and safe.

The very first print copy of this book was raffled off to support The Young Center, and won by a fellow author, Kelly Maher.
I matched her winning bid with my own donation.

ABOUT THIS BOOK

For the first time ever in print, Zoe York breaks down how she plans a series—something she has done ten times over. Romance Your Brand is an adaptation of an intensive four-week course, now available to authors everywhere. This book covers:

- high-concept pitches
- taglines and blurbs
- world building and casts of characters
- writing the first book in a series
- finding comparable series and covers
- how to write towards future marketing
- and why ALL OF THE ABOVE should be considered before you write a single word

"Genre fiction series are the bread and butter of mid-list writers. For many they make the difference between a writing dream and a writing career."

ABOUT THE AUTHOR

Zoe York is a thirteen-time *USA Today* bestselling author of contemporary romance, often with military heroes, and always with scorching heat on the page. Between her two pen names (she also writes erotic romance as Ainsley Booth), she has published more than fifty books since her 2013 debut, *What Once Was Perfect.* Notable career highlights include *Prime Minister* (*USA Today* bestseller twice, in 2016 and 2017), the *SEALs of Summer* anthologies (*New York Times* bestsellers in 2014 and 2015), and the fan favourite Canadian small town series, Pine Harbour and Wardham. She is a mouthy and proud member of Romance Writers of America and Toronto Romance Writers.

facebook.com/zoeyorkwrites

twitter.com/zoeyorkwrites

instagram.com/zoeyorkwrites

youtube.com/zoeyorkwrites

ACKNOWLEDGEMENTS

I'm grateful to Nikki Haverstock and Rosemary Rey for their thoughts on early drafts of this material. I need to also acknowledge the fifty guinea pig colleagues from RomanceDivas.com who took my one-time-only class in 2016. Their questions and thoughtful participation was invaluable feedback as I developed my thoughts on what makes a successful genre fiction series.

Thank you as well to Kim Cannon for her fast proofreading. Any remaining ellipses errors and all superfluous "So…" are my own error and/or ridiculous editorial choice.

For years, I've said I don't want to write a non-fiction book. Obviously, I'm a liar.

I love to talk about writing and publishing. I love speaking to others, in groups large and small. Workshops? Yes please—as an attendee or as the presenter, I'm not picky. And then there's Twitter, and Facebook, and my every-so-often threads on the state of publishing as I see it.

But deep down, I know those thoughts are transient. There's a lot of moving parts in publishing. A lot of advice that is old before the ink fades.

And yet...

A few years ago, I gave the following text as a luncheon address in the suburbs of Boston, at the annual conference of the New England Chapter of Romance Writers of America. It's about watching my mother do desktop publishing from our kitchen table in the 1980s.

There is some advice which stands the test of time. This book is my offering in that regard. Time will tell if it's solid or not. I hope some of it is useful to you, and you take that and do something great with it. The rest, feel free to discard. Most of the time, I'm flying by the seat of my pants anyway.

———

Three things I want you to know right off the top.

1. I'm nervous, and that's okay. Joanna Bourne reminded me that this is a good thing—it's my body preparing me for the hordes to advance with pitchforks.
2. Should that happen, I'll just turn it into my next Vikings in Space adventure, so that's all good, too.
3. Everything I know, I learned from those who came before me. I would be lost without this community. And when I

remind myself of that, I'm not nervous anymore.

It's an honour to be asked to give this lunch talk, and I was thrilled to be asked. The committee has truly done an outstanding job organizing this conference. The quality of the workshops has blown me away. So like, no pressure, Zoe. But this is my first keynote-type address! And I want to get it right.

Just like when you sit down to start a new writing project, the possibilities are endless but also overwhelming—do I share something poignant? Go for the funny? Be motivational?

The thing is, when you're handed a microphone, and you're a bit of a maverick like I am, you start to think...is this the only time I'll ever get to do this? I have to say all the things!

I still feel like my eight-year-old self, that eager little girl who has discovered a love of novels. I was raised by a single mom, and we didn't have a lot of money. I got to buy two new books at the Scholastic Book Fair each year, and the rest of the time we bought books by the bag-full at yard sales. I went to the library every week and signed out ten books at a time, and when I returned them, I stood at the counter and talked the librarian's ear off about my favourites. That is still who I am in so many ways.

My mother taught me a lot—about readers and publishing, about money and running a small business. She was a journalist, and wrote about parenting and family life for newspapers and magazines. And after she had her third child, my brother, she struck out on her own, and started an independent parenting magazine, because she kept writing articles no editor wanted to print. Radical articles about attachment parenting and breastfeeding. In the early 1980s, that just didn't sell.

But deep down, my mom knew there was a market for that. She wanted to read that kind of magazine, and even though it was scary, she was willing to bet there were others who did, too.

She didn't have the internet. She had trade shows and word of mouth. Her newsletter sign-up form was a clipboard and instead of MailChimp or Aweber, she used child labour, and had me and my sister collate the magazines into bins for the post office. Most five-year-olds don't know that Canadian postal codes go from A on the east coast to V on the west coast, but I did.

That was my first lesson learned in publishing.

My second was that mailing lists and fanbases

grow one name at a time. That there's no real shortcut, and the most valuable names are the ones that are scratched onto a clipboard list after a real conversation.

Today we've got the internet. And we have online forms instead of clipboards. But it is still authentic interactions that build a true fanbase—reading an amazing book or meeting an author online or at an event like last night's book signing, and something just clicks.

And when I finished my first romance novel, thirty years after watching my mother forge her own path, deep down I knew I would find readers with it, for it, directly. I knew indie publishing was for me.

When I started to write this speech, I racked my brain—what is the nugget of truth that I want you to take away? What can I dig out of my experiences in the wild west of indie publishing and share with you that's both actionable and easy to digest? How can I inspire you to take that brave step to do something new and exciting, that might make all the difference?

And I came up with a few ideas. But the problem is, the ideas I came up with seem to contradict each other.

That's often how it is in publishing.

We are told **it's a marathon, not a sprint**, but then

when an opportunity drops in our lap, we need to write like the wind for two weeks flat-out on the off-chance that this might be our big break.

We're told **they want unique voices, something fresh**, but also familiar and recognizable.

We're told **write the story of your heart**. And write to market. [Bree Bridges, one of the two writers behind the Kit Rocha duo, has solved this one for us. She says, "write the most commercial story of your heart", and that's exactly right. That's what we should do. Figuring out how is a whole other thing.]

We're told to **take chances and invest in ourselves**, but the money should always flow towards the author.

We're told **not to give up**, but also to consider starting over.

The truth is, writing is hard, and publishing is a brutal business—and not always a meritocracy. To survive, and thrive, you need to be tough. You need to believe in yourself and trust your gut. You need to see through smoke and mirrors. You need to shut out all the noise, and find your own path.

But it's just not that simple, because that takes resources and support. You need a solid platform in life in order to get a really good leap. I know that.

I struggle with the reality that there are a lot of

asterisks on good advice. Mental health, physical health, financial stability, access to opportunities—they all factor into our ability to do what someone else has done. Publishing is a weird formula nobody has ever quite figured out, and privilege weighs heavy.

Success takes a lot of hard work. But it also has something to do with the position you start from. And privilege is often called luck.

I grew up poor. That's a disadvantage. But my mother was a trailblazer in indie publishing, long before the internet. That was major advantage for me. I learned some lessons as a child that made me look at traditional publishing through a very different lens.

It is tempting for me to tell people, **this is what you should do.** But the reality is, **I don't know if it is.**

So now, with some asterisks firmly in place, let's get to some possibly good advice.

———

We come to conferences like NECRWA because we recognize that this entire enterprise is hard, and we want to be professionals. We want to get it right. Writing, publishing, networking...there is a lot to what we do. **Of course it starts and ends on the page, with characters who become real to us and stories we're**

desperate to tell. But we know that the business of publishing is bigger than just creating compelling stories, and we know that a lot of it will feel like walking a tightrope.

We all struggle with balance. If you're one of those people who find it a challenge to switch between wearing your author hat and your marketing hat and your publishing hat or your contract-negotiating hat. Maybe even your mom or wife or roommate or daughter hat. It's hard to figure out how to keep writing when we're pulled in all different directions.

As I said, when I first agreed to speak to you, I thought, I want to talk about **stepping outside of your comfort zone**.

I know that the lessons I've learned definitely point me in that direction—stepping outside my own comfort zone has been when my career has leapt forward.

But after the high of a new release that's done well, there's an inevitable crash that follows. Not enough people talk about this—all books become backlist.

All sales slide. And riding that rollercoaster can be disorienting.

The real lesson I've learned is that balance is the key, and I don't mean that like some kind of Zen thing. Real balance is a wobbly, dangerous gymnas-

tics feat that requires fearlessness and a laser-like focus locked on an unmoving point in the distance.

You need to take risks, and you need to play it safe.

Not at the same time.

What I've learned is that publishing is a zig-zagging kind of industry. Opportunities here and there, left and right, sometimes zinging past so quickly we miss them. Don't worry about that. There will be another opportunity. But if you are too rigid, you will miss more than the flexible person over there who's just hooked a new deal. And if you are too flexible, you'll lag behind your goal-oriented friend over here who's writing book eight in a solid-but-slow-earning series.

The most common question I get asked by other authors is, "How do I brand my book? How do I brand this new series? I have this great idea, how do I make it a hit?"

And the honest answer is, "I have no idea."

Truthfully? I don't know how to make *my* next series a hit.

And if you're thinking, whoa, Zoe, this is not the way to give a keynote address, you might be right.

But I'll tell you how I weather that unknown.

My biggest advantage when I started publishing

was that I knew it would be hard. That I knew the path would be bumpy and there would be failures and missteps along the way, and I just needed to keep my eyes on the prize, in the distance.

I was lucky to find a professional community, full of women with diverse experiences and an eagerness to share the lessons they'd learned. **When someone shares their journey, pay attention. There's so much there for us to learn from each other.**

The three most useful conversations I had before I published my first book were:

1. A wide-ranging comparison of debut book sales in the first month. Wide-ranging is really important here because some people will have amazing launches—and there are some good lessons there, too—I'll get to that in the second point. But the biggest takeaway I learned before I published anything was that most likely, my first book would sell somewhere between twenty and a hundred copies in its release month. I sold forty.

2. How series can make all the difference when marketing genre fiction. Again, there are exceptions to this, standalone books that

soar. But the consensus among the experienced authors I talked to, who had the careers I wanted, was that their bread and butter sales came from an extended series. Five or more books in a common world, each one about a different couple. And for most of them, those series came later in their career, after they'd have some trial and error of launching and pitching and promoting their books. **Some people nail all of that on their first go, and have a debut success. These people almost always have paid attention to the lessons that others have learned through trial and error. (I paid attention, but still didn't have success out of the gate. That's okay, I was expecting that).**

3. The best book you'll write is way down the road. I remember this conversation really clearly. The question was, "What's the best book you've written?"—and while a lot of the authors I looked to as mentors did have answers along the lines of, "I really liked this book, it's my favourite to date," almost all of them shared the mindset that their BEST book was yet to come. **That kind of**

thinking is really conducive to forward momentum. And in genre fiction, where a successful author will write ten, twenty, thirty or more novels in their career, it's almost essential.

The corollary of all three of those points, while not necessarily spoken out loud, became cautionary tales I internalized.

1. Don't expect success out of the gate; just write the book and move forward.
2. Don't give up on a series because of weak sales; the series will eventually drive better sales.
3. Don't get caught up in how awesome your first book is; the next ones will be even better.

I don't believe in trying to write hits. I believe in writing about the characters that clamour loud in my head, the stories that make me zing with excitement on the inside. I believe in writing them as well as I can, and bleeding blood onto the page in the process.

In front of you today are some of my books. I chose these novels because they are representative of the path I took to success. It was bumpy and it was uneven. But it was also, at all times, quite clear to me.

What I want to talk to you about today is a couple of things, and they all loop back to this question of **how do I do this? How do I figure out my path to success?**

The answer really is twofold:

First, you push yourself out of your comfort zone, and you find something that sizzles in your bloodstream.

Second, you come up with a five-year plan that allows for some flexibility, and you stick to it. Commit to yourself and commit to that project that makes your heart leap.

And when I say a five-year plan, I mean this in a rolling, revising general kind of way. When I was practicing this talk, my assistant asked me where I'm at in my five-year plan. I stopped and looked at her, and said, "Day one. Always, day one."

Now, if I've done this correctly, right about now, I'm tweeting about this talk. If you're on Twitter, check me out, I'm @zoeyorkwrites. I tweeted a picture of a chalkboard, and there's a big circle in one corner of it. That's your comfort zone.

And way on the other side is a dot, with an arrow

pointing to it. **Where the magic happens**, reads the caption.

> Your comfort zone over here.
> Where the magic happens way over there.

What exactly that means for you is going to be different than what it means for the author sitting next to you. Everyone's path is different; when to hit publish, when to start a new series, when to start over...nobody can tell you what the right next step for you might be, except for you. And right now, I hope you're starting to get a kernel of an idea. It might scare you.

Hopefully it scares you! That'll tell you that you're on the right track. Trust that idea. Let it drag you out of your comfort zone and magic will happen.

I know this is easier said than done. Trust me when I say, I've been there.

Like a lot of authors, the first book I started writing is in a trunk somewhere. Mine is a digital trunk called Google Drive, and there it shall languish forever. It's terrible. It was followed by many more failed first chapters, first acts, standalone scenes. I spent a lot of time and energy writing a story I knew deep down inside, one that was near and dear to my heart.

I want you to think about your own first stories. The ones in the trunk, and the ones you've finished. For me, those books were reflection pieces, in a way. The first one I actually finished, **What Once Was Perfect,** is one of the books I shared with you today.

I love that book. It's the book of my heart in so many ways. It is also completely inside my comfort zone.

A Viking's Peace is another passion project, that's really my happy place as a writer. Totally inside my comfort zone.

It took me four books to first write something that was a little outside my comfort zone. That book, **Fall Out,** is also at some of your spots. That was my first Navy SEAL romance. I wrote it for the SEALs of Summer military romance superbundle. For those of you who take that copy home, I encourage you to read it—and notice how, at points, the story could be stronger. I'm the first to admit that book isn't perfect. It was written on a deadline, with very high stakes. I had to make it into that boxed set; I knew in my heart it was a huge opportunity to reach new readers.

But I was definitely out of my comfort zone, and the writing was hard.

I was literally dragged through that book by Anne Marsh and Kimberly Troitte. I sent it to them in pieces when it was about three quarters done. I wasn't in a good head space with my day job, and I thought the book was awful.

They told me they loved Drew and Annie.

For all its imperfectness, that book, written far outside my comfort zone, created two very memorable main characters, and their passion for one another was much stronger than what I'd previously written.

I stepped out of my comfort zone and magic happened. This is definitely true for a lot of writers, and I think there are a lot of reasons for it. We have to get creative in order to cope with stress and disorder, so when we step outside of what we know, what we've always done, we...try harder. We apply our craft more vigorously. We are more comfortable with the idea that we don't know what we're doing, really, so we're way more open to feedback and instruction.

I wasn't aware of any of this happening. I was scared and full of doubt.

When the SEALS of Summer bundle released, it soared to the top of the charts. That boxed set hit the New York Times and USA Today bestseller lists. And I got a huge injection of new readers who had fallen in love with Drew and Annie.

I desperately wanted to retreat to my comfort zone. The last thing I wanted to do was write another SEAL book.

I think that's probably the pattern that most writers take. Write some safe projects, that appeal to our hearts and our loyal readers, and then take a risk. We can't constantly be writing on that edge, because sometimes risks don't pay off. Sometime we leap out of our comfort zone and land in muck.

But the day after SEALs of Summer hit the NYT list, I was laid off from my job.

And let me tell you, there's no bigger reality check about what you write and how you write than suddenly having writing shoved from a part-time passion to a full-time responsibility.

I gave myself six months to turn writing into a job that could replace my previous career.

I looked at my long-term plan for my series, and I looked at my brand.

I asked myself, what do I need to do here to **appeal to my existing readers (some of them having been my readers for all of one week at this point).**, and what can I write that won't feel like tearing out my finger nails.

That's how I came up with the idea for Pine Harbour. Small town romance, but with military heroes. The first novel I finished in that series is another one that I brought for some of you. *Love in a Small Town* was the first book I wrote with both commerciality and longevity in mind.

It was the first book I wrote with a piece of my heart and a lot of my brain.

Writing it was a joy, but also a job.

***Fall Fast* and *Prime Minister*, which is written under my alter-ego's name, Ainsley Booth.** Every book I've written since has been written in a fundamentally different way, because I am now a fundamentally different writer. I am a commercial genre fiction writer in a way that I was not when I started.

When I strictly wrote the books of my heart, that were safe inside my comfort zone...there is nothing wrong with those books. I love those books. But they're commercially weaker.

And that's the real lesson I've learned. That balance thing is so important. But it's easy to say, and not so easy to do.

Writing and publishing often feels like we're walking a balance beam. If we worry too much about where we are right now, if we let ourselves drop our gaze and stare at our toes, we'll stumble.

Keep your eyes on the future. Think about where you want to be a year from now. Five years from now. What books do you want to *have written*? What series do you want to be known for? Set that plan in motion today.

Know that it will take you some time. Know that it will be scary, and there will be bumps in the road. That doesn't matter. Because you are committed to that future you. You aren't worried about your next step, you've got your gaze glued on the horizon. You're already thinking about a **five-year plan full of brave new steps.**

And look around you. This is your squad.[1] **We can support each other with our experiences, our missteps and our successes. And we can remind each other that this is a long journey, and we are not alone.**

———

I gave that speech in early 2017. What follows in the rest of this book is an updated version of a course I built in late 2015, delivered once in early 2016, and then put in a trunk because teaching a course is a hell of a lot of work, and I prefer to spend my time writing books.

I promised you the truth, didn't I?

But as I said at the top of this foreword, I love to talk about writing and publishing—not just because I'm a data and process nerd, but because there's nothing I love more than helping someone find the information they need to get to the next level of success.

If part of your five-year plan is writing a series, then hopefully this book is part of that information you need.

---

1. Full disclosure: when I gave this speech at NECRWA, I used the word tribe here. For publication, I've edited it to say squad, because when you know better, you do better, and modelling self-correction is a good step to helping others know better, too.

CHAPTER ONE

BUILDING A MARKETABLE SERIES

NOW A BOOK, OR LET'S CALL IT A DIY WORKSHOP

"GENRE FICTION SERIES are the bread and butter of mid-list writers. For many they make the difference between a writing dream and a writing career." That's the epigraph to this book, and it's my entire raison d'etre in the sphere of workshops, presentations, business chatter, and the odd conversation random strangers find themselves trapped in with me.

As I explained in the forward, I didn't set out to write books for a living. I had a career I loved, and writing was a part-time pursuit. I did it professionally, but casually. And then I was laid off—the day after I first hit the bestseller lists. And I hit them in style. Number six on the combined New York Times list. Number twenty-two on the USA Today list.

There's a lot of potential in those numbers.

They're also a flash in the pan. You're a star for a week, and then sales slide. They always slide. All books become backlist. You'll hear me say that again!

But it was both a sign and an opportunity that these two moments in my life—becoming redundant in academia and hitting the bestseller lists in fiction—happened within twenty-four hours of each other. I wasn't going to pass that up, but I was going to move forward in a smart, career-focused way. I was going to write series. I knew that in my core, because of the lessons I'd learned from other writers before me, for all the reasons I will spell out in this book.

Much of the content that follows was once delivered in a four-week intensive course. My first effort to share what I learned from others and pay it forward. Now I'm thrilled to offer it in this book format.

But writer, I don't want you to miss the fact that this was once doled out in chunks over an entire month! So please take your time with this and do the work in pieces. Each person has their own right schedule, but you don't want to rush the series preparation period. That's when you get the most important parts right—or wrong.

No pressure!

But seriously, it's worth letting yourself have the

space to consider all the options. One of the best pieces of advice I've heard from people teaching courses is to try to apply new learning to a new project, rather than one in progress. I'm going to pass that same advice on to you now. You will be tempted to retroactively apply what I talk about in this book to your existing work.

Don't do that—at least not yet.

I know what it's like to have a strong impulse to fix old projects. I'm not going to tell you never to do this —that would be hypocritical of me. I tinker all the time. The power and privilege of self-publishing means that I can add a new first chapter, or change a title to make it more appealing to a cold audience. I've done both of those things. They've moved the needle a bit, for a moment.

What has always moved the needle more significantly, for a prolonged period of time, is starting a new series. And then, once I've found a chunk of new readers that way, there is even more value in bringing them into your backlist with a polish and scrub on that older material.

So, if you want to level up, I encourage you to first focus on building a brand-new, bigger and better series from the ground up. The lessons you will learn along the way will help you even more when you go back to the messy job of fixing what is already "done."

On that stressful note... In this book, I'll cover the following topics:

- publishing in a digital landscape
- high-concept pitches
- taglines and blurbs
- world building
- building a cast of characters
- writing the first book in a series
- finding comparable series
- covers
- and why ALL OF THE ABOVE should be considered before you write a single word

By the end of this book, I hope you have a clear idea of where your planned series will fit in the genre fiction canon. You'll have a robust cast and a big world designed that can accommodate many books.

To that end, I want you to plot out at least five books in the series arc. And by "plot", I mean titles and hooks/taglines, maybe even covers—no actual plotting for this pantser[1], but if you want to go to that depth, that's cool, too.

We're going to do all of this built on a foundational

understanding of how the digital publishing landscape works, and what some basic marketing principles are. Once you have your series planned and have begun writing it, then you may want to do a deep-dive into more complex marketing plans in my next book, *Romance Your Plan.*

But first, you're going to write.

That's always the best advice: write the next book. Or in this case, write the next series.

I'm excited for you. Let's start by covering the basic difference between ebooks and print books distributed by publishers through physical bookstores.

---

1. I'm leaving this line in, as is, but the truth is that I'm not really a pantser. I'm more of a quilter, a term introduced to me by Tamsen Parker. Which is to say that in 2016 when I first wrote some of this material, I thought I Did Not Plot Anything, and it turns out I was wrong. I plot in a wild, write-many-random-scenes-until-a-plot-emerges kind of way. So if you think You Do Not Plot Anything…be open to the possibility that in fact you do, in a way unique to yourself. We don't always have objective distance from our own processes.

CHAPTER TWO

EBOOK PUBLISHING

THIS CHAPTER COULD DATE REALLY HARD, REALLY FAST

MAYBE ONE OF the reasons why I said I would never write a non-fiction book about publishing is the fear of putting something down in print...and then it fading into history, a relic fact from days of yore. Or 2019, which will basically be days of yore before too long.

So, with all the usual caveats of who-the-heck-knows what fun twists and turns our industry will take in the next decade, here are the important elements of ebook publishing I think all authors should understand in order to build the most marketable series.

Writing standalone novels obviously has a significant place in a publishing career. But in fifty-

something books, I have yet to do that. It's just not my area of expertise.

In part, that's because I've focused on the ebook market.

When a book is intended primarily for print distribution, it can't be too obviously part of a series, because there's no guarantee that the other books will be shelved beside it—and indeed, there's a solid chance they won't! Print paperbacks all need to look like standalone stories, unless they're numbered as part of a trilogy or must-be-read-in-order series.

And even then, most of those titles being acquired today are from experienced authors who have delivered in that model before, or the one-in-a-million lightning strike book that goes to auction.

If you are writing that kind of novel, this book isn't for you (right now).

I say that without any judgement. There are many different publishing paths. I'm a right-down-the-middle-of-my-genre type of genre writer. I want to write a bunch of books a year (anywhere from three to eight, depending on what else is going on in my life), and I want to keep doing that for many years to come.

This book is for people like me, with wide margins on either side of that description. Slow writers?

Welcome. Fast writers? Get in here. Careful writers? YOU TOO. Reckless, risky writers? Of course.

Anyone who wants to focus on a digital readership market—either self-published or with a publisher that has strong digital sales focus[1]—that is, anyway who thinks their primary audience is in ebooks: those are the people for whom I am writing this book, because that is where my area of limited expertise is.

But once we hover there, in that spot—writing genre fiction for the ebook market—I can confidently say I know what I'm talking about. I have started ten different series, and written more than fifty books between them. Everything that follows in the next chapters is based on the lessons I learned from other writers in the early days, and from the mistakes I've made along the way trying to implement their wisdom.

One reason authors with a digital audience (those of us who self-publish particularly, but also anyone who has had long-running luck with a digital-first publisher) preach about series is because of how reader discovery works.

And here is where authors often get hung up. **I'm going to warn you not to say, "but that's not how *I* discover books." You are not anyone's ideal reader in a commercial author/reader relationship.**

Most authors are the *least* likely person to discover a new-to-them author and glom an entire backlist. Why? Because they already have their favourites, and they have a To Be Read (TBR) pile a mile deep. Also in this tough-to-please crowd are bloggers and reviewers.

So set aside yourself, and any other professional reader, and let's think about the reader discovery process.

The analog book discovery process is often tactile. In a bookstore, at a yard sale, on a friend's bookshelf. Browsing, touching, picking up, turning over, looking inside. So much of how we crafted books in the past is based on this assumption, and how *some* books are crafted today are still rooted in this assumption. Any book that is being aimed at a singular book buyer for a major retailer, for that Holy Grail of a fifty-thousand copy print run…this is their bag.

It is not mine, and it is not likely to be yours. (Or it may be for a few books, but not forever).

The digital reader cannot hold a book in her hand. They do not particularly care about the length, or the typesetting, or the back cover copy[2]. They don't benefit from the little tiny details on a cover or splurging for gold foil and raised text.

(This isn't to say covers don't matter: they do, a lot,

but in a split second gotta-grab-them manner, not in a luxurious perusal kind of way).

Also, the digital reader **can see in an instant** (hopefully) if a book is part of a series, and should be able to access all the other books in that series with a single click. More on this in chapter six, because **Metadata Is Important**.

The digital reader is also likely to be loyal to her digital library source, usually the retailer where she buys the books, and may connect with other readers who consume the same kind of books.

And of course, there are lots of digital readers who don't fit any of the above descriptors. There are lots of casual readers in the digital landscape, too, those who only read a handful of releases a year, leaning heavily on the bestsellers that get a lot of buzz.

For what it's worth, I have found there's a lot of fierce competition for those eyeballs, for that buzz, but elsewhere in the readerscape there are lovely spaces to be found that are way less competitive.

One way to build a solid career is to focus on the newish-to-e-reading voracious readers who can read much faster than you can write, who are happy to gobble up your backlist when they discover you.

This means writing in series, which are the easiest way to promise readers that the next book is similar to the last one. Genre fiction readers sometimes want to try something new, but most of the time want a fresh take on a familiar and favourite trope, theme, story or protagonist archetype.

We like what we like. And when we get a taste of it, we want more. Ebook publishing is uniquely suited to delivering that.

---

1. I don't have any opinions on one publisher over another, but in general, I think it's smart to put your ear to the ground and find out what the writing community in general thinks of a publisher before you consider signing a contract with anyone.
2. I have a whole chapter on back cover copy: Chapter 9, Blurbs In the Digital Age.

CHAPTER THREE

THE SALES PITCH FOR WRITING SERIES

AND MY FAVOURITE F-WORD

THIS BOOK IS part sales pitch for series (they work!), part coaching (because writing a series doesn't come naturally to everyone), and part boot camp (to help you make your series tighter, stronger, and closer to your ideal product).

The audience for this book is a writer who aspires to be (or to continue being) a prolific commercial genre fiction author. We publish books to find readers. A series will help us find readers because one book leads into the next; if we can hook a reader, they will carry on and gobble up the rest of the connected stories.

This **connection** is what we can leverage in

marketing. The most accessible to authors marketing options are free and 99 cent funnels from a loss-leader book to the rest of your titles. But those funnels only work when the books share a common promise, and ideally, a common cast, setting, and themes. In short: a series.

How long should your series be? This principle works on a duet or a trilogy, but really starts to pay off when you have five, six, seven, or eight books connected by metadata, with enough titles that you could plan out a whole year with an alternating quarterly schedule of backlist funnel, front list release, backlist funnel, and front list release again.

And maybe you already know that, which is why you picked up this book. So, eyes on the prize: you want to write a marketable series. ***This means book 1 will, eventually, be marked down to free or 99 cents, either permanently, or off-and-on via temporary promotion.***

If you are writing for a publisher, when this discount happens might be out of your control. But you should expect that it will happen at some point, even if your publisher currently doesn't discount books. They will. It's the new world order.[1]

It's also great.

I love giving books away for free. At the moment, I have eight books available for free, out of my catalogue of fifty-something books.

The power of free in the marketplace is variable. It's entirely possible that you have tried a permafree first-in-series, and it didn't work. Your face is all scrunchy now, and I get it. **It hasn't worked for some of my efforts, too.** *That doesn't mean that it never works. It means it didn't work on that project, at that time, on that retailer.*

When you have fifty-something books released, that's a lot of comparable data. And I have noticed fascinating non-trends in my free trials.

The top free book in my catalogue is different on each retailer. The top performing free book on BookBub is different again from any of the retailers. Every market of readership is slightly different, and it shifts with time as well.

But within that variation of success (from a barely there blip to a soaring spike in sales across an entire series), there is this undeniable truth: it's always worth trying. If it works, awesome. If it doesn't, then that's a learning experience. Maybe the covers were wrong for the category, maybe the sell-through potential isn't clear to readers, maybe the blurbs are dated, or off-trend for the genre.

Please don't be so stubborn that your first attempt at pitching a series is the final effort in that regard, no matter what. Be humble enough to know that you may need to keep trying to figure out what effectively delivers the message you want to be sending.

In chapter ten, I do a deeper dive on what the first book in the series should look like, but a quick word about length right up front. You don't want your first book to be too short (and probably not too long). Ideally it will be a short novel, 50-60k-ish. Why?

Three reasons:

1. Novels have a longer half-life than novellas and serials. You will be able to promote the series longer, and see more evergreen sales from a "full" story. (Apologies to all short story writers, you are amazing, never doubt that fact.)

2. Some powerful marketing options (cough, BookBub[2], cough) have a stated minimum length of 50k words. (Note: They also say 150 pages, and we all know those two things aren't the same. I have a 45k short novel that they take almost every time I ask [*What Once Was Perfect*], so the 50k thing isn't a hard and fast rule, but a good guideline.)

3. 50k keeps the pacing tight, page-turn-worthy, and in a digital landscape, that's important. Longer is not necessarily better for a digital reader.

And there are other marketing efforts that I want you to have in the back of your mind that also work for both backlist funnel and front list releases:

1. cross-promotion (boxed sets, similar indie authors, etc.)
2. newsletter (you have one, right? If not, stop reading right now and set one up right now)
3. formatting your front and back matter for ideal reader capture and connection

What I am not going to talk about at any point is advertising. Ongoing digital advertising is only one aspect of a marketing plan, and it requires time and money. A lot of writers don't have much of either, and I do not believe advertising beyond limited, targeted promotions is necessary to build a successful genre fiction series.

If you write a series that sells through itself, you don't need to work as hard on the finding a new-to-

you audience for each new release. **And for people who do not naturally gravitate to marketing and advertising, who would prefer to hole up in a writing cave, the long series can be the answer to their publishing aspirations.**

So, to be clear: marketing needs to happen, but what you write can reduce that workload down the road, if you design a series that is geared toward the most basic elements of marketing: zero barrier to entry, easy to access fandom world, connected stories in a familiar world.

I want you to have this mantra in your head: *I will write a marketable series in my favourite genre.*

Which of course begs the question: what genre is that?

Homework:

Write down a list of potential genres and sub-genres you want to write in. Which ones are scary to write down? Which ones make you excited?

1. I wrote this paragraph in 2016. It's even more true in 2019.
2. This is one of the moving targets of publishing that I worry

may date badly after I release this book, but from 2013-2019, crafting a book to be "BookBub-able" has remained solid gold advice. As the kids say, YMMV.

CHAPTER FOUR

COMPARISON IS THE THIEF OF JOY

A QUICK WORD here about the risk of looking at comparisons when figuring out where your book sits in the marketplace (because that's where some of us go when we start to think about if our books are urban fantasy or paranormal romance—we look at where other books are shelved).

An essential business skill is being able to put on your marketer hat, look around, look at the marketplace...and then take off that hat.

Writers don't need to have other people in their head when they're writing. You do need to understand the market, but only in the same way you need to understand craft—it'll make you a stronger writer. But the rules aren't the boss of you, you know?

At times in the past I slipped into a space of being frustrated that "nobody wants to read sexy small town Canadian romances about smart women." There's a lot to unpack there: it's a problematic way to look at my own books. Most romances are about smart people— that's not as unique as I think it is when I'm down on my sales.

But the truth that I realized was, it's not that people didn't want [insert how I see my books]. It is that they ALSO wanted:

- a recognizable community
- archetypal leads
- tropes
- high-stakes
- hooks into the next book

None of that is at odds with what I was writing. It just wasn't explicitly in the packaging of what I was writing, and maybe not strongly enough on the page. (No maybe about it, but hey, we can be gentle on ourselves. "Is Wardham a prison?" is a question I've been asked more than once. My next small town series is set in a place called Pine Harbour, though. I learned.)

Comparison is often the thief of joy. Don't let that happen.

When thinking about the genre, don't get too hung up on why X book is selling well compared to yours. Instead, stick to looking at your own book, and be real with yourself about where it diverges from the best parts of the genre standard conventions that you love.

Do your market research, vent at me on Twitter if you want (but know that I'm probably going to turn it around and ask you questions to get you pointed in a positive path), and then figure out **what you want to write**. *That's what this is all about*.

An Urban Fantasy world is inherently, if subtly, different from a Paranormal Romance world. Erotic romance is different from New Romance (what I call New Adult-esque books that are really about adults but with that fresh, first person voice) which is different again from Contemporary Romance.

It's okay if what you write bridges two genres, as long as it satisfies both sets of readers. That's a tall order; an advanced move, if you will. I found it easier to write small town romance, and military romance, before writing small town military romance, for example. Nothing wrong with a practice series.

Nothing wrong with aiming high right out of the gate, either! But a series that falls short of its goal is frustrating for writer and reader alike.

CHAPTER FIVE

WHAT IS A SERIES, ANYWAY?

A SERIES IS a set of connected books. That's it. In the next chapter, I go into what metadata is and how it's everything in the digital landscape.

A trilogy? That's a series.

A set of standalone novels about different protagonists, but set in the same world? That's a series.

An ongoing series of stories about the same protagonist? Obviously a series. But not the only one!

A duet? Yes, that's a series! But it's a short one.

When it comes to book universes, length matters. But just like in life, series of all lengths and sizes have their place. Yes, that's a reference to...exactly the thing you might expect a romance author to make a reference to.

A long running series is where fandoms will truly flourish. Shorter series, or even standalones, are often easier to grab cold audiences with a really hooky lede or trope. Lots of authors alternate these with good success. But if you've only ever written trilogies or shorter, and you've picked up this book in the hopes of learning how to build a bigger world that can sustain many, many stories, I'm glad you're here.

Author and psychologist Jennifer Lynn Barnes has done a lot of research in the area of fandom, and I hope in future editions of this book I'll be able to point to her published writing craft books on this—but for now, let me just say, look her up. She has spoken at writing and publishing conferences I've attended, and each time I've come away with a significant shift in how I understand readers and how they engage with the works we produce. In this territory she is the expert and I am the rapt pupil.

Many prolific writers pen multiple series inside the same common world. This is, ideally, where you are heading. In this new series you build, you will hopefully find new readers, and as you write, new series. The question of when to spin off into a new collection is one that vexes all of us. And the answer lies, most likely, in what you want the metadata to look like, and how you want those books arranged on the digital storefront. Where do you want the reader discovery to begin? With multiple series in a common world, you have multiple first-in-series entry points—which is great if you think you can hook new readers better with a new book one. But if you break up the world into too many silos, then reader discovery can stop, and only true fans will carry from one collection to the next.

CHAPTER SIX

METADATA

"IT MEANS DATA ABOUT DATA" (I KNOW, THAT DOESN'T CLEAR ANYTHING UP)

I'M BREAKING this out into its own chapter because this is technical, and I don't want the details to get lost in the more creative fray of building your next genre fiction series.

But after I talk about metadata, I want you to set this information aside, okay? You'll come back to this chapter when you're ready to publish the first book in your next series.

SERIES NAME

Something I say to a lot of authors who have started a series, maybe they have two books out but they look like standalone on the retailer storefronts, is "Make sure your books are metadata linked." And it's the number one piece of advice I get follow-up questions on.

What does that mean? It means that when the books are published, the exact same information (data) is put in the series data field. If two books by the same author have the same (the exact same! I cannot stress this enough) information in the series field, the various ebook retailers will (should, anyway) link them automatically.

It looks something like this:

> *Between Then and Now* (Wardham #1)
> *What Once Was Perfect* (Wardham #2)

And then on the book page, there will be a hyper-link (which is a clickable link) to a search results page for all books that match that series descriptor.

One common problem I see is in the middle of a long series, the publishing data is wrong on a single book, like this:

> *Between Then and Now* (Wardham #1)
> *What Once Was Perfect* (Wardham #2)
> **Where Their Hearts Collide (The Wardham Series #3)**
> *When They Weren't Looking* (Wardham #4)

In this example, the "series page" on most retailers will stop at book 2, because book 3 looks—on a data level—like a different series. And most retailers require series numbering to be sequential, so book 4 then becomes an orphan.

What does this mean for reader discovery, as discussed in the last chapter? It stops at book 2.

The good news about digital publishing is that errors like this are correctable, either directly on the portal where you published the book in the first place, or if that fails, polite and persistent follow-up with customer service.

But series names are not the only important piece of metadata to consider when planning and building a genre fiction series.

SERIES NUMBERING

These rules vary from retailer to retailer, but in order to be consistent, let's follow the series numbering rules of the most stringent retailer (Amazon): in order to be linked properly, each book must have a whole integer number. No 0.5s for the intervening novellas authors like to write in between novels. Unfortunately, this problem is hard to reconcile once stories of varying length and significance are already written. So before you start planning your next series, please consider *not* writing a prequel novella or any 0.5 episodic stories in between novels.

"But Zoe, I love those stories!"

Reader, so do I. I'm writing out of experience here, I promise you. But my prequel novellas and .5 wedding stories about couples who had their own books were completely *invisible* on the retailer fronts as a part of a series.

Going forward, I won't be writing them anymore in expectation of them selling on the retailer in an ongoing way.

What are the exceptions?

- A limited edition holiday story
- A limited edition prequel that won't need to be leveraged in an ongoing way
- A story written for your website, newsletter, Patreon, fan club, and offered up as a hook in your published books' back matter

If you have written a number of short stories adjacent to a main series, you can also think about linking those stories together as their own series. We did this with the Frisky Beavers series, packaging the short stories as Frisky Beavers Quickies. That's not my ideal front list publishing model, but it works as a way to make lemonade from lemons, so to speak.

CATEGORIES AND KEYWORDS

Categories are the broad "shelves" you pick, often (but not always) tied to BISAC codes. The big genres have sub-categories you can get down into, but then keywords can trigger even more niche lists on some of the retailers.

There are some good tips that I've learned over the last three years with regards to categorizing your books properly, and some popular myths as well.

Myth: Ranking higher on a sub-sub-sub-genre list will help with visibility

Truth: Not really. I mean, maybe, with the ten people who happen to look at that sub-sub-sub-genre list that month, but what are the chances they notice you as they scroll for whatever it is they're specifically looking for that drove them to click all the way deep into Amazon's lists?

Readers find books by word of mouth, from recommendations on trusted sites/email blasts, on social media, and *sometimes* by browsing in a retailer.

So the categories, genres, sub-genres, keywords,

etc. matter, but not as much as you might think. That being said, if you only connect with one or three readers by improving your categorization and keywords, and they love your book and tell five people, it'll have been a good use of an hour of your time.

Some retailers have themes and search refinement tools that aren't in every category, but if they are in yours, they are more valuable than random keywords. **THESE SHOULD BE YOUR KEYWORDS.**

If this is something that you struggle with, spend some time on the storefronts. Start with a keyword search you think you'd use for your books, and see what that first string delivers you. Click into the most comparable title to yours and see where it is shelved. Rinse and repeat a few times until you have a few consistent categories scribbled down.

Ideally, you want to get your book into BIG, MEDIUM and SMALL categories.

EXAMPLE:
romantic suspense (but you can pick this BISAC category, so you don't need it in your keywords as well)
Sci-Fi romance (same as above)
science-fiction, fantasy, **superheroes, Amazon,**

female protagonist, warrior, adventure romance
(if you have more than 7 keywords, you can string a few more in there with OR: **science fiction or dystopian or post-apocalyptic or survival, fantasy, superheroes, Amazon, female protagonist, warrior, adventure romance**)

The key takeaway I want you to remember about metadata as you move into designing your next series is that metadata needs to be machine readable and machine searchable. Content on your cover needs to be in metadata fields as well to be found by readers. Most retailers don't include content from the book in any search results—don't bury the lede on what your story is about! Make sure your book description, title, subtitle and keywords carry all the weight there. And finally, keywords that are too random, and series names that don't link, don't turn your individual titles into the findable genre fiction series readers are looking for.

CHAPTER SEVEN

WORLD-BUILDING AND CASTING

IF YOU DID the homework from chapter three, hopefully now you have a clear idea of what genre you're building a series inside. If you still don't, that's okay, but know that you want to sort that out before you do too much work, because that's the foundation. Every genre has tropes which help with world building, both in guiding your stories closer to what readers are expecting, and helping you subvert those expectations in the most delightful and unexpected ways.

In this chapter we're going to talk about what gets built on top of that genre base:

- **world building**
- **building a cast of characters**

The next step in building a marketable series is creating an accessible, fascinating world with a robust cast of characters that readers want to follow.

Some writers start with the world, and others start with the cast. It doesn't matter which one *you* start with, but like with the genre, I want you to have the basics of both of these pretty clear before progressing forward, because if you are too focused on one and not the other, it can impact on marketability.

If you start with your Characters, and build out to the World, you might run into some problems. Like you really want your heroine in book three to be a librarian, for example, but you've already established in book one and two that she didn't finish college and has worked at her parents' grocery store ever since. You can fix it by sending her off to school again, but that might annoy your fans who want her to settle down and have babies. And by you, I mean me, and Wardham #2.

In gaming, they call this **bottom's up world building**. If you start with a careful creation for your world, then fit in people, that's called **top down world building**. The risk there is that we end up with stories that are set in a beautiful, detailed world...and everything is already in place, without any conflicts or problems. So you bring in external drama, which works in some genres better than others.

The best stories are probably created in the middle, in a tornado of ideas and maps and celebrity inspiration pictures, with nothing set in stone until every part makes sense and there's conflict vibrating off every surface.

Or that's the goal, anyway.

WORLD BUILDING

Some of this is just for your own reference, and will remain invisible to the reader. Some of it will be shown to the reader. All of it needs to be consistent and interesting. Familiar helps, too. Three factors to consider:

1. The Physical World

Your readers won't be able to visualize your world with ease if you don't have a complete 3D image in your head. And preferably, also written down/drawn out, so you don't forget it (or so it doesn't shift over time!).

HOMEWORK #1: I want you to draw a map of your world. It doesn't need to be fancy, and it doesn't need to be a literal picture. It could be a pencil sketch of a town, or a rough outline of a star map. Just a list of ranches and small towns in the rural area of your Western romance series, or a street that will be at the heart of your big city romance. Maybe a floor plan of a police station or skyscraper. This is strictly for your own work, and if you've already done something like this, pat yourself on the back and call it done.

---

2. World Interactions

This is more about the laws of your world. If you're writing contemporary romance, you have it easier in some ways at first, because you can just use the laws around us. EXCEPT... not all your readers live in the same state/country/hemisphere as you. So you have to be aware of the assumptions you're making. Same with if you're writing in an alternate world, with magic and shifters and rules that have been in your head so long, they make total sense to you. **You want to run your world through a Global Sniff Test.** *Can the average anywhere-in-the-world English-reading adult understand the world as presented? What needs to be explained?* **Can it be explained in an interesting and** *fundamental-to-the-story kind of way?* This is a big question, because world building and explanation can drag down the plot and interfere with the reader getting into a character's head.

3. The Existing Canon of Your Genre

Regency romance, space opera science fiction, cozy cat mysteries...there are existing canon rules readers love (and some they are eager for writers to mess with). A lot of these are subtext beneath tropes and protagonist archetypes—the rake, the rogue pilot, the plucky amateur sleuth.

HOMEWORK #2: What will be familiar in your world to avid readers of this genre? What are your favourite recurring bits? Jot that stuff down on a list! We'll refer back to it later.

BUILDING A CAST OF CHARACTERS

Let's talk about those dynamic characters who will drive your stories:

PROTAGONISTS

Broken man, haunted past. The hero's journey. Reluctant fighter. A meet cute that changes everything for someone on the wrong path in life. Your main character is someone who is, for whatever reason, not in a Great Place, and something needs to happen for them to get there (hopefully with some struggle and learning along the way, plus some entertaining happenstances for the reader to enjoy).

In a romance, you have two (or more) leads, and they both (all) need to be compelling, but that can be in different ways. One protagonist could be closer to an ideal, a fantasy, another could be someone the reader can identify with and almost slide themselves on top of, put themselves in that character's shoes.

In a mystery, you've just got the one protagonist, and so they really need to be a combination of both. Relatable but also heroic.

And then around them, the secondary characters. I don't write bad guys that often, so for the craft elements of writing an antagonist, you'll need to look elsewhere, but if that's your jam, they need to be solid, too. For a romance, or really any genre fiction because we all love a good spin-off series, **the secondary characters might one day become protagonists**. So you want to pay attention that you craft them in a way that people will say, "**When is Dean's story coming out?**"

It doesn't take much. A line or two. Some space in your world building that creates mystery about

their past and questions about what their future might hold.

Homework #3: Write out your cast. Just their names for now. Again, we'll use this later. Maybe keep that list in the same place as you have your favourite trope-y elements.

How are you feeling about your series idea now? Any shifting going on? (Have you had an idea for a different new series? That happens to me sometimes when I work through this set of exercises!)

By now you should be thinking about how your series fits into the market, and be mindfully considering what the cast and world look like. World building is something that people do entire workshops and books on. Same with crafting really solid characters. The key points I want you to remember in relation to building a marketable series *is that the world should be familiar and recognizable to the genre reader* and *the cast introduced in book one should make people ask for the next book based on the characters alone*.

If you have that in your mind as you write the first

book, you're already going to be ahead of the average writer.

In the next chapter, we'll cover pitching your series (and your first book). And the first person you need to pitch it to? Yourself.

CHAPTER EIGHT

THE PITCH

HOW YOU SELL YOUR BOOK—TO an agent, an editor, a reader, the media—is all essentially the same thing. An elevator pitch, a high-concept proposal, tag lines and blurbs are all trying to do the same thing: capture the essence of an idea and promise it has broad appeal.

You gotta know your hook, is what I'm saying. And it's easier said than done.

Let's pretend I have a time machine and can have a conversation with myself.

Full disclosure: the first time I wrote this was in 2016. 2016 Zoe still had some learning to do. **The 2019 additions are new.**

2016 Zoe: Tell me about your series

2012 Zoe: I love sexy small town romance, so I want to write that. But set in Canada.

2016 Zoe: Okay, sounds cool. Sexy small town romance, got it.

2012 Zoe: But set in Canada.

2016 Zoe: Uh-huh, I got that part. That's cool. Tell me about your heroes.

2019 Zoe: Just saying, the Canadian angle could be a good hook. Don't ignore that.

2012 Zoe: The first book is about a female plastic surgeon who left her small town, and her first boyfriend, to pursue her career. Now they reconnect over the holidays.

2016 Zoe: And the hero?

2012 Zoe: He's a teacher.

2016 Zoe: Alpha? Amateur boxer? Play hockey at least?

2012 Zoe: Hmm. He likes sci-fi novels and video games.

2016 Zoe: Well, at least you're an eternal optimist. So what's the pitch?

2012 Zoe: I really wanted to turn the whole doctor hero/teacher heroine thing on its head.

2016 Zoe: Can you sum it up in a high-concept "this meets that"? What is it comparable to?

2012 Zoe: It's not really like anything. Maybe Jill Shalvis, if her heroes were teachers who played video games and lived in Canada.

2019 Zoe: Think outside other books. TV show comparisons?

2016 Zoe: Yeah, we need to work on that pitch. Tropes?

2012 Zoe: First loves! Reunited lovers! Second chance romance! ***sags in relief that she had at least that***

2016 Zoe: Okay, second chance at their first love...roll around in that for a while. And maybe make the next hero a boxer or an NHL player.

2012 Zoe: Got it.

2016 Zoe: You will eventually. ****gives self a hug****

2019 Zoe: Not so fast, girl. One day you'll get more nuanced on that whole alpha hero thing.

See how much work it is to rework an older project, aka, talk sense into your former self? I still love this first series, but shifting it around to make it slightly more marketable has always proven more work than just writing a new series. Trust me, I've tried.

Which is why I now try to work on my High-Concept Pitch before I write most of the book. Or any of it, for that matter.

PITCHES + HIGH-CONCEPT IDEAS = HIGH-CONCEPT PITCHES

A pitch is a single sentence description of your project. A high-concept idea has mass appeal, originality, and places itself squarely in the zeitgeist.

So a high-concept pitch is the combination of the two: **a single sentence description of the core of your project, identifying the part of it that has mass appeal, originality, and places it in the zeitgeist**.

Not all projects are high-concept, and that's okay; if the series you're working on doesn't suit this exercise, set it aside for a second and play around with high-concept ideas for your genre. Even if you can *approach* high-concept, that works.

LIKE:

- A new twist on an old favourite (The Cowboy's E-Mail Order Bride)
- An unexpected combination of two tried and true ideas (Snakes on a Plane)
- Taking something to the next level (Vampire band of brothers but they're HUGE and totally badass, aka Black Dagger Brotherhood)
- Go big or go home (Series of contemporary romances about siblings falling in love; each sibling is at the top of their profession—a movie star, a baseball player, a business man

—or a fan-favourite archetypal job, like a librarian or firefighter, a la Bella Andre's Sullivans)

- Put the trope right in the title (Pippa Grant, Lauren Blakely, Helena Hunting all do this so well! Fresh and funny. Or outside romance, look at James Patterson, the king of marketing...who worked in marketing for two decades before he started writing)

HOW TO GET STARTED:

- Make a list of the tropes in your book; this will expand on the list you started in the previous chapter
- What's at the CORE of your story? What's the conflict at the start of the book?
- What are the occupations of the MCs?
- Where does it take place?
- What's the twist?
- What has the BROADEST APPEAL?

There is nothing wrong with writing a niche book. But *marketing* a niche book, as a niche book, is damn hard. So if you can find the widest possible marketing device for your book, you're much more likely to find readers who like it.

HOMEWORK: **From the list of tropes you've jotted down, which have the widest appeal to the readers of the genre you've picked?**

Bonus points if you can actually work up a high-concept pitch for a book to-be-written, but that might take a few days. Right now, I just want you to start thinking about this as you refine the series set-up, world and cast.

This is tough work that you are doing!

I want you to remember this: I'm never going to tell you that you're wrong. This is my book, with my goals and objectives. I put it together because I saw some gaps in my own series design, hindsight being 20/20 and all that, and wanted to pay that forward. But most of the time, for any of us, it's a crapshoot.

The most powerful writing tool you have at your disposal is your gut. **Do gut checks often. Trust what you feel inside. Including, sometimes, the little squiggly worry that you might not know how to do something.**

Develop a circle, a network, a loop you can turn to when your gut check tells you that you need a different perspective.

But your stories are already inside you. I don't want to convince you to write something wildly different (except one of you, who secretly wants to write a not-them-at-all project—you should write THAT, I promise!).

So do that gut check now. And then sleep on it. Unless you're reading this early in the day, and then mull on it as you go about your business.

CHAPTER NINE

BLURBS IN THE DIGITAL AGE

AND BY "BLURB" I MEAN BACK COVER COPY, NOT A QUOTE FROM YOUR FAVOURITE AUTHOR

AS AN INDIE-FIRST AUTHOR, I sometimes use a different vocabulary from my traditionally published author peers. Historically in publishing, a blurb has often been used to describe an endorsing quote from another author—added to the cover, or used in other ways in marketing.

But "the book blurb" has also come to mean **the back cover copy**, and in chapter two, I made the scandalous statement that readers don't care about this in digital in the same way they do in print.

I stand by that statement (obviously, or I'd have edited it out of the book). Now I'm going to double down on it. But I'm also going to clarify what I mean: readers don't care about a full three paragraphs of (hopefully compelling) book summary or introduction.

They may eventually, so it's not bad to write a traditional chunk of back cover copy. At the very least, you can use it on your actual back cover of the print copy!

But on most of the ebook retailers, as well as Goodreads and other book-centred corners of social media, readers only see the first paragraph, or maybe a tag line and part of the first para.

That's it.

(And yes, reader, I have tons of three paragraph blurbs on my books. It's hard to follow my own advice sometimes.)

But the most important bit of "blurb revision" we can do is to that first line or two. We have one second for the right keywords to jump out and promise a reader, *this is exactly what you are looking for*.

The good news is, if you've already worked on your high-concept pitch, you already have the bulk of this work done. How does your blurb look if you simply put that log line in bold at the top of the book description? A big improvement already.

The next step is to rework that pitch into a blurb that ends on a hard tease, that makes a reader one-click because they simply must know what happens next. Create questions they cannot walk away from, and make them buy your book. Don't worry if it doesn't look like back cover copy "should." The only thing that matters is if it resonates with readers in the audience you are targeting. And if it doesn't? Try again.

CHAPTER TEN

THE FIRST BOOK IN A SERIES

THE FIRST NOVEL in a genre fiction series is an opportunity to find new readers and reinvigorate your base—if it's what they want to read (on both counts).

Before I was a (professional) writer, I was a reader. Life-long. I adore cozy mysteries, romance of almost all genres, sci-fi, thrillers, and post-apocalyptic stuff as long as it doesn't involve zombies. We all have our limits.

[Funny story: my husband writes and draws zombie stories, and sometimes I beta read for him. That's true love.]

When I think back to the series that I have glommed[1] in the past, that I still remember, I see a lot of the same elements that I see working in bestselling books today.

Even being able to recognize that, I couldn't put all these elements into my first two first-in-series books. And I'm not sure why I couldn't. One of my CPs told me to—she's super smart, obviously. But it just wasn't what I wanted to *write*.

This is something that I see over and over again, now that I've had the benefit of time passing, and can be slightly more objective about my 2012 self. When I sat down to write my first books, I wrote my favourite parts of what I'd been reading: sizzling chemistry and smart dialogue. Tenderness. Man, I love to read about tenderness, between couples and between family members, too.

But tenderness is more of a moment, not a complete story. In itself, it doesn't sell books to a broad audience.

A good story:

- is high stakes
- is about a journey
- is larger than life
- has a strong but flawed protagonist
- has the main character learn something the hard way

- has turning points
- raises those high stakes even higher toward the end
- has a really serious low moment (feels like death, might actually be pretty darn close to death, depending on your genre)
- has a satisfying denouement, made even more so by the strength of the lowest-of-the-low point

This is seriously a do what I say, not what I do thing, because I *still* struggle with my all-is-lost points. My fourth Pine Harbour book, my editor was like, "Do you just not want there to be a black moment in this book? Because you're at book four. You can take it out. But you can't pretend this little fight is a black moment."

DAMN IT.

I rewrote the last quarter of that book because I'm not a weenie. And that's the series that I'm trying really hard to get it all right on!

So I bet there's something that you shy away from. Maybe you don't like the larger-than-life romance hero, tall dark and handsome, with broad shoulders and a six-pack who can also cook and is good to children, but he's brooding, and has secrets and won't share them. (I don't know why, that guy is AMAZ-ING). But even if you don't, I want you find a version of him that you do like, because if you're writing m/f romance, THAT'S PROBABLY WHO YOUR FIRST HERO SHOULD BE. Some version of him. (Here is where deft subversion comes in handy, too, but it must be deft).

Or maybe it's the journey that you struggle with. Find the right starting point—don't be afraid to chop off the first three chapters of your book. Or add three more chapters at the end.

I want you to get the first book right.

And then I want you to make it free.

That's the other thing you should have in your mind when you're writing book one of a new series. *At some point down the road, I'm going to strip all barriers to entry, and give this thing away to EVERYONE. Which means people who don't love this trope or even this genre are going to give it a try. How many 1-stars on my lacklustre journey or weak hero do I want?*

Knowing that you will eventually make a book free changes the way you write it.

As it should! And it will also mould it in different ways, too. Don't make it too long. 50-70k is plenty, even if you're planning the rest of the series to be longer.

It should be long enough to be a satisfying read, but leave lots of hooks and questions about the world and cast so the reader is compelled to pick up the next book. All that world building and casting that you did in chapter seven is not all going in the first book. Not the details. (Unless maybe in fantasy! Those readers like that sort of thing.)

HOMEWORK: I want you to think about a book in your genre, first-in-series, that you remember from a while ago. Not one that you read in the last month. What do you remember about it? What made it stand out in the field? What elements were trope-y and familiar?

At this point, it's worth reminding ourselves that missing the mark isn't a failure. It's a learning opportunity. And nobody hits the mark every time. Anyone who teaches a course, writes a book or a blog post, and tells you what worked for them is probably leaving out what *didn't* work for them.

And those things that worked for them? There are dozens of people, who aren't running a course or writing a book, for whom the same thing didn't work.

The truth is, success is found in trial and error. There's no magic button, and maybe everything I've taught you so far might not be quite right for you.

I still think it's all worth trying.

Through trying on what's worked for others, you will find what works for you. And when it feels like it's your own special sauce, your own magic button, that's probably when you've found the ticket to a successful series.

So what did *I* do at first? I've mentioned some of the mistakes in the Wardham series—Wardham is a made-up town name that fits into Southwestern Ontario (or maybe New England). There's a town near me named Wingham, for example, and just across the road in Michigan there's a Wadhams Road. In my own world view, it sounds like a small town. Not to readers outside my immediate area, though. This is why it's important to beta test everything, and read things out loud. Have your best friend read things out loud. If you have a reader group, post some different options and see what reactions you get. (This is what I did, and my readers named my next small town series Pine Harbour.)

I also went with an unconventional couple having a reunion romance for the first book in the series. Sweet and refreshing for die-hard contemp romance fans, but not with enough mass appeal to launch a series. And at the end of the book, they end up in Chicago. Not the small town. I also started the book with the heroine heading home for Christmas, having just broken up with her co-worker, who was an occasional friend with benefits.

For three years, I knew deep down none of that was what the largest segments of the market wanted. At first I didn't care. It was my story, and I was going to tell it as I saw fit. Then I cared, a little, because other books did better, and that book is the book of my heart. Then I didn't care again, because fuck 'em, my story, and *some* people really like it.

Then I had an epiphany. I saw a new first chapter, in the hero's point of view. I wrote it in an hour. Then I added it to the book, went through and edited in a few other things here and there that matched it, and the book felt SO much better. After two and a half years. How about that?

That opened the flood gates. I've since written two more stories about them getting married and having a baby and moving back to a (nearby) medium-sized town with a hospital (she's a surgeon), because you know what? Life is too short not to make people happy. I write romance. HEAs, with all the bells and whistles, that's what people want.[2] And so I'm giving it to them, exactly as they want it.

2012 Zoe is cringing a little. She'll get over it.

The other series where I stumbled is SEALs Undone, which despite that has done pretty well. **How did I err here? I didn't know the first book was starting a series. Or at least not THIS series**. I wrote it for a boxed set, and planned it to be a Navy SEAL novella that would introduce a romantic suspense series about a group of international mercenaries. But then I decided *not* to write that series, and do a SEALs novella series instead. Except *oops*, I didn't introduce many SEALs in the first book, and none as obvious sequel bait.

So book two in that series is really the starting point. For both Wardham and SEALs Undone, I find that I have to make both books 1 and 2 free (alternatingly and sometimes together) to hook people into the series. Later-in-series books have also been made temporarily free at times. Not impossible to recover from, but it means more marketing, more effort, etc.

---

1. My copy editor, Kim Cannon, suggested this might be better as glommed onto, but that's not how I described consuming an entire series. I just glom it. So I stetted this note, and am

grateful that non-fiction allows for endnotes to explain my idiosyncrasies.

2. Your readership might not want babies and weddings, and YOU might not want that, and that's okay. This addition felt right for me and this book and this series.

CHAPTER ELEVEN

PUT YOUR SERIES IDEA IN AN ARRAY OF COMPARABLES

IT'S ALMOST time to start writing. Almost.

First, though, I'd like you to put your series in a line-up. Yes, just like on a police procedural show. But instead of hoping a reader can pick yours out of the line as the one (as in, the one that doesn't fit), you're hoping that yours looks like it fits just right in that other company.

Find five other series, put yours in the mix there, and test your elevator pitch against the others. Is your idea high-concept enough? Could the world be tweaked? The cast be tightened, or expanded? Are you hitting the same kind of beats that readers connect with?

Does your series name make the same split-second genre promise as the others? Or could it be called something else, maybe something else that tags a keyword or two? You want to be wearing your marketing hat for this exercise, not your writer hat. Don't be precious.

And then do it again with the cover concept. **But Zoe,** you might say. **I don't have my covers yet!** We'll get to that next.

COMPARABLE SERIES

As I mentioned in the forward, there's a lot of competing advice in the publishing world. **Write to market, but make it fresh and original** is the two-fisted disorientation here.

Let me clear this up: don't overthink what you're doing. You are going to write *your* stories, the best way you can. You're just going to be a bit mindful of the market when you go to brand and package them. Got it? That's all we're talking about here. Don't throw out the baby with the bathwater.

Another way to do this is, instead of wearing a marketing hat (if that stresses you out), put on your publisher hat instead. Ask yourself, "If I were an acquiring editor for my own publishing house, would I acquire this project from another writer?"

If not, why not? What needs to change about the project in order for it to be ready for market? Don't be afraid to give yourself a revise and resubmit note!

And when you get that note from yourself, take it seriously. If your series, as pitched, doesn't fit next to the series it should—based on how you've presented it —then you have two choices. You can make it more like what you want it to be, or you can find a new spot in the market. Find new comparables. They're surely out there! Sometimes what we read and what we write are sufficiently different that we're blind to other areas of genre fiction. There's no shortcut here, unfortunately. It's research time. Dig into Goodreads, poke around on the retailers, using all the keywords you think you might ever use for your new series idea.

And keep going until you do find the right comparables. They are out there.

This might be a bold thing to say, but I don't think you're the first person to have this general series idea, whatever it is. That's not how genre fiction works! And that's okay. The sooner you get comfortable with the fact that we're in the business of reworking the same five ideas in our own way, the better off you'll be

... there's nothing that interferes with being productive more than righteous outrage over being copied. Reader, it's not worth it. I promise.

Now, every so often we do get ideas that feel pretty original. You might wonder what my thoughts are there, if you've found a series idea that truly *isn't* like the others you would stack them next to. With the important caveat that this is less common than we all think it is, I'll acknowledge that every so often this happens. Writer, if it makes your blood sizzle, I want you to tackle the project with full enthusiasm. There's a lot of potential there to make a corner of the market your own. But it will take more marketing effort to find your readers, so plan ahead for that. (Hey, I'm going to write an entire book on that next, so let's loop back to this conversation then!)

COVERS

In the same way as it is easier to sometimes pitch a concept than a finished book, it is also easier to commission your covers early in the process, before you get too picky about what the art looks like, because in the book it's *just so*.

My number one plea of authors who are struggling

to connect with readers in their preferred genre is to engage the services of a cover artist who makes those exact kind of covers. Not your sister, former co-worker, or someone who will barter you for copy edits...unless what those people can do is exactly the same as a professional cover designer.

And I say all of this as someone who does my own covers. (So obviously, I include you in the last paragraph, if you are a DIY cover artist. Do you, boo, but do it well, or else.)

As we are publishing in a digital landscape, it is also important here to pay attention that we select comparable covers from that same digital landscape. Scour the ebook lists, not bookstore shelves.

If this is an overwhelming task to take on for a series that doesn't yet exist, try it on an existing series (if you are willing to consider a rebrand). This runs counter to my earlier advice to not try to mess with something already done, but I think for covers, it's all right to make an exception. Here's a secret: publishers change their backlist covers regularly if an author is still selling. So we need to do that as well.

So what does this line up look like? Literally like a snapshot of the top books in your genre. It's a fun game of cut and paste! You can use the example mock-up I've made (download the image at my website, www.romanceyourbrand.com/your-book-here/)   or actually take a screenshot of your preferred retailer's top list for your genre—but you'll still want to cut and paste other covers in there, because you want this comparison to be *tight.*

Once you have the other covers picked out and in place, drop in your cover.

I want you to be as objectively critical here as you

can. Make a list of any element that is unique to your cover, that isn't seen on any of the other covers you've picked out. Note all significant differences in the major three parts of a cover design:

1. Art or images
2. Title typography
3. Author name brand

Please note that I talk about the two sets of words on the cover quite differently. The title? That's typography. But your name is not *just* typography. It's a brand stamp, and you want the font treatment there to be more iconic, something that could carry across all of your books.

After you list all the differences between your cover and the rest, make a second list—everything that is common to at least two of the images on the page.

These two lists are the starting point for you to work with a cover designer, or someone in-house if you are fearless, and get the cover design just right.

Every year I pick a target word or a motto for myself to help me stay focused on my goals. In 2015, my phrase for the year—a year in which I was completely focused on lifting my business to the next level, without any deviations or distractions—was, "Don't be different, be better." Out the other side of that year came this chapter, and I hope it gives you some food for thought on branding and packaging.

CHAPTER TWELVE

MIDPOINT REVIEW

SO TO THIS point in the book, we've touched on the following points:

- the marketable structure of a genre fiction series, including tips for a first in series
- the importance of balance between world building and the cast of characters
- high-concept pitches and blurbs in the digital landscape
- finding the right comparable series and covers (don't settle for not-really-comparables! They don't help you!)

Next, we'll take the first steps to actually writing

some of that first book! Let's bring those characters to life in that magical world you envision. We'll also talk about consistency and writing tools that really help in crafting subsequent books in a series.

HOMEWORK #1: Before you start writing, do some reading. Pick up a new-to-you first-in-series novel.

Pay attention to the moment when you realize, there's going to be more than just this one book.

For me, I think of Virgin River by Robyn Carr. The first book, the hero is a stable, strong, handsome, Marine with secrets and a good smile. But he's got another Marine working for him, and Preacher isn't a conventional book boyfriend[1], but somehow I knew as she wrote him, *how* she wrote him, that he would get the next book, and I was insanely curious about how that would go.

A Princess in Theory by Alyssa Cole is another great example of sequel bait all over the pages. Both of the protagonists have a secondary character beside them (a best friend for the heroine, and an assistant for the hero) who have clear They Get a Book, Right? questions created on the page as soon as they're introduced.

Homework #2: After you see this in action, give it a go. I'd like to have you work on a scene or chapter. Maybe the start of the book, or a scene after the action subsides if you start with action, where you show the reader the world they're going to spend the next 5-10 books in, and tease them hard on what is surely going to come next.

---

1. As I did the proofreading for this book, Netflix debuted the TV series version of Virgin River. That's a good alternate bit of homework if you'd like an excuse to sink into the show—it's excellent—but Preacher is significantly different on the show. He's more talkative and definitely more conventionally attractive (they cast a super hot actor!).

CHAPTER THIRTEEN

EXCERPT WRITING

WELCOME BACK! I hope you actually took a bit of a break after the midpoint review and did some reading. And maybe you started sketching out a scene, as I suggested in the previous chapter:

I'd like to have you work on a scene or chapter. Maybe the start of the book, or a scene after the action subsides if you start with action, where you show the reader the world they're going to spend the next 5-10 books in.

Writing an excerpt like this is also great preparation for marketing a series, and getting a media kit together for a book. I'm doing that right now[1], and picking excerpts is really hard. One way to fix that is to write some of the excerpts in advance.

I can hear linear writers howling at me. Don't worry, you don't *need* to write them out of order. For you guys, you'll need to wait until you've started at the start and moved into the book. Maybe until you've finished the first draft.

THEN, you'll pull a key moment, and polish it up into an excerpt.

It took me forever to connect the fact that an excerpt didn't have to be word for word from the book...and that if I couldn't find a chunk that worked as an excerpt, maybe some of my chunks needed to be tightened and re-inserted into the book.

Food for thought, right? This is the core of what I'm talking about when I say that **marketing starts with the product, and in order to sell books, you need to write books that sell.** Get this right, and the rest gets that much easier.

In this second half of the book we'll also circle back to the casting and world building topics, because there are layers there that really help with marketing, too.

And finally, I'll also talk about consistency and writing tools that really help in crafting subsequent books in a series.

———

HAVE you ever read a snippet of something and thought, "Holy hell, I need to read more of that?" Try and remember a time like that, and figure out what it was about that excerpt that hooked you. **Chances are, it was a single line.** On most retailers, readers who want to get a full sense of your writing style can download a sample or look inside the book, just like they can in a physical bookstore. So your first chapter needs to work as a really long excerpt. **But all other excerpts should be more tease than description. More seduction than sample.**

Think of how movie trailers are made. Scenes are spliced out of order to give you an idea of what the movie is about without giving away the story. They're designed to make you want more, to make you think *you are missing out if you don't see it*. This is the gold standard for book teasers and excerpts, too. At the end of an excerpt, you want someone one-clicking.

I like to see an excerpt **end in a moment that leaves the reader hanging**. This usually means ending sooner than you think.

It's good if it can stand alone without any setup, too, that the average reader can infer the setting and character details from the snippet, so **they immediately feel they know what's going on**.

Another good way to focus a snippet is so that

it **screams your genre**. Think of this as a second piece of the same homework. First I want you to think about an excerpt that shows your characters, but when you nail that one, move to a second one that shows your genre. For a romance, this means an excerpt that crackles with sexual tension. For a mystery, show the sleuth being clever. For a comedy, show that it's funny. For a thriller, scare the pants off us.

And for a long-running series, it will also show the world that it's set in.

---

1. It doesn't matter when you read this, I'm probably still trying to get stuff together for a media kit. Nobody tells you that grabbing links and excerpts becomes a forever task in publishing. So hey, let's talk about media kits...

CHAPTER FOURTEEN

MEDIA KITS

ONE OF THE reasons I've never been great at keeping all the important information about a book together in one place is that I don't like the term "media kit." Maybe it was a visceral reaction to the marketing aspect of publishing, when really I just want to write great books and shove them out into the world!

So obviously, I had to write a chapter on media kits, because like them or not, they're great.

It really helps if you start at the beginning of a project, keeping a pull file of the log lines, teasers, excerpts, blurbs, trope lists, etc. that we talked about in the first half of this book. All of it. Why? Because anything that resonated with you as you planned the book might be great marketing material down the road, and you can only use it if you can access it. If it's lost to the ether, that does you no good.

Different length excerpts or different kinds of hooky materials work best for different platforms. Twitter loves a list of tropes, preferably paired with appropriate matching emoticons. Instagram is photo heavy. Facebook loves a medium length snippet. Your newsletter is a great place for a longer excerpt (or your blog, don't forget about the real estate you fully control!).

So as you work on this new project, save it all: the polished chunks, and the rough, raw things you love the most about this new series. Copy all of it into a single file somewhere. Name it Book Title Media Kit, even if you're like me and the term Media Kit gives you hives for reasons you can't quite figure out. This will help you find it again, down the road, when a blogger asks you if you have a media kit—and then it's an easy term to search for in your computer. I'm sure I'm not the only person who loses files, right?

Here's an example of a basic media kit, which you can also download from my website at www. romanceyourbrand.com/media-kit-template/. It's not an exhaustive file by any means.

MEDIA KIT FOR [TITLE]

LOGLINE

Series:
Author(s):

BUY LINKS (full):

Apple:
Nook:
Kobo:
Google:
Amazon US:
Amazon UK:
Amazon AU:
Amazon CA:
Amazon DE:

BUY LINKS (shortened):

Apple:
Nook:
Kobo:
Amazon*:
Google:

* some people use a redirect link for all the Amazon stores so you only need one link here
instead of all of them

BLURB:

SHORT BLURB:

EXCERPT #1:

EXCERPT #2:

EXCERPT #3:

TROPE LIST:

THIS MEETS THAT COMPARISON:

In addition to what I've got here, you can also include:

- links to Goodreads and Overdrive
- links to your paperbacks[1]
- links to audiobooks if you produce those
- Keywords as you think of them, to help you with that metadata piece when you go to publish

LINKS

I have the links for my ebooks listed twice, because a stack of short links is the easiest thing to share on social media. Those links don't get truncated, which means bloggers and readers can copy and paste it easily, and the links don't split across lines. But most of the promo blast opportunities, such as BookBub or Freebooksy, will want the full links, without any affiliate details or shorteners on them. And if you are focused on building a series, with backlist promotion down the road as part of the publishing plan, you'll need those full links over and over again for years to come.

If you haven't used link shorteners in the past, I use smarturl.it. I like that I can change the link underneath the short link. Genius links are another option, especially if you are interested in running a lot of social media ads and want the granular tracking detail. I'm not a detail person, but some people are! And there are plug-in options for websites as well, if you prefer to keep that kind of thing on your own site (especially if you want to use affiliate links, which most retailers require be used on your own platform and not masked). Redirection is the plug in I hear people recommend the most often for this purpose.

———

AND THAT'S the media kit! Doing this will also highlight what elements of your marketing package are missing. Again, this is one of those "acquisition editor" moments. If you were a publisher, and acquired this project from another writer, what would you have your marketing staff put together for them? **If you were that writer, newly acquired, what would you want your publisher do for you?**

In self-publishing, you are that publisher. If your "publisher" doesn't pull their weight in putting together marketing materials, have a talk with them.

———

1. Paperback links you might want to consider including: Indie-Bound, Book Depository, Amazon, other major bookstores in your country if they stock your book online (more likely if you distribute with IngramSpark than only via Amazon).

CHAPTER FIFTEEN

ENTHUSIASM: THE UNDERVALUED FACTOR

ONE REASON I'm giving you worksheets and tools in this book—other than to be helpful, hopefully—is to show you the value of systems[1].

And I say that as a completely disorganized, impetuous, hotheaded artist type. Publishing is a wild rollercoaster of emotions, and they can get the better of us. They can convince us that we need to make a change when we don't (every panicky last-minute 99 cent sale) and stall us out from making a decision when a new direction is desperately needed.

Emotions are a problem.

Which is ironic, because enthusiasm is a published author's greatest strength, and it can feel a lot like tapping into your emotions: harnessing your favourite parts of publishing, for example, the things that genuinely thrill you and make you happy.

The key word there is harness. This is why, despite my artistic nature, I love systems and lists and plans. They provide some natural boundaries and remind me where my enthusiasm is helpful (and when it's wildly off base).

As I said in the foreword, every day is day one of my five-year-plan. No system will ever constrain me, and I like nothing more than reviewing and revising what I'm doing and where I'm going. But what I want to avoid—and what I want you to avoid—is the negativity spiral, the doubt and second-guessing which can derail a very good plan.

To that end, I want you to use some of the work you've already done to make the world's simplest mission and vision statements, and an action plan. Don't panic! I'm only using those words to sound fancy. I promise you, you've already done this work in previous chapters.

Take your research into your favourite genres, your answer to what ideas fill you with fear and excitement, and add on top of that the list of your favourite tropes, sub-genres, character archetypes, etc. The funnel result of those things is your next series idea. Stay focused.

TAP INTO YOUR ENTHUSIASM

1. Mission: Who you are, what you write, and maybe who you write it for. YOU AND YOUR GENRE.

2. Vision: WHAT YOU LOVE. Your favourite tropes, sub-genres, archetypes, and story structures.

3. Action Plan: Put THAT ON THE PAGE. Nothing else. Harness your enthusiasm and write exactly what you want to write, in the form that is most compatible with commercial fiction.

THAT ON THE PAGE

WHAT YOU LOVE

YOU & YOUR GENRE

ROMANCE YOUR BRAND
MISSION / VISION / ACTION PLAN

TAP INTO YOUR ENTHUSIASM EXERCISE

1. Mission: Who you are, what you write, and maybe who you write it for. YOU AND YOUR GENRE.
2. Vision: WHAT YOU LOVE. Your favourite tropes, sub-genres, archetypes, and story structures.
3. Action Plan: Put THAT ON THE PAGE. Nothing else. Harness your enthusiasm and write exactly what you want to write, in the form that is most compatible with commercial fiction.

When I shared this exercise with my friend Nikki Haverstock, who writes humorous mysteries, she said, "It's easy for me to trick myself with a shiny idea but then I step back and say, 'Do I really like this long term?'"

Yep—that will shine a spotlight on what you really want to write. This is an exercise you will want to do over time, with revision. Don't laminate your first draft...which is excellent publishing advice in general.

The other thing we talked about is finding the

sweet balance point between what you love and what the market loves. If you are a commercial genre fiction author (beat that drum again, Zoe), then one of your goals is selling books. Simple as that. You need to consider what the market responds to. I strongly believe that the most relevant data here comes from your own catalogue, rather than watching the market at large, unless your strengths lend you to true writing-for-hire type creativity.

But once you do that analysis (my small town books sell better when they have military heroes), and you write it down as a vision for your brand (the middle part of this exercise), then you need to trust that framework and not do too much subjective second-guessing as you get into the nitty-gritty of writing.

One example from my own writing, as Ainsley Booth, is the specifics of how erotic the text can get. Many times I have found myself caught up in fear of being too filthy. Is a specific sex act a turn-off for the average reader? What about my readers who have found Ainsley's work via my Zoe catalogue?

But "transgressive sex acts" are literally on my id list. They make me happy to read, and to write, and they're core to my voice. When I reassure myself of that, by looking at the list I wrote down at a different time, the panic and doubt ease. This is who I am. I'm never going to please every reader.

Did you just feel that right in your chest?

You, too, writer, are not going to please every reader. Stop trying to. Stop constraining yourself, and start writing with enthusiasm only. Write the jokes you want, the action you want, the tender moments, too.

Do it within the genre convention standards! But once you understand those, this is where that delightful subversion comes in.

It's finally time to start writing.

---

1. The value of systems is not equal to everyone, or universal. I've done a lot of work with Becca Syme, author of *Writer, You Need to Quit*, and I highly recommend her QuitCasts on YouTube for figuring out what works for you and what doesn't. So when I say that systems have value, I mean, you need to figure out the right system for you!

CHAPTER SIXTEEN

WAIT! LET'S MAKE A QUICK WORLD AND CAST CHECKLIST

IT'S okay if you started writing at the end of the last chapter. But at some point (and for a lot of authors, this might be after the first draft), I want you to run through a quick checklist on your world and cast.

Once upon a writing time, a group of authors were talking about making our worlds big enough for a series of books. My author friend, Melissa Blue, threw out an awesome question which simplifies and focuses a lot of the world building in contemporary settings (but also applies to all other genres as well):

- **Is there a main place in your story where folks can gather?**

Coffee shop, commons room in a college dorm, a palace, some kind of headquarters, a garage where they all work. What location grounds the World? Does it have a memorable name, is it described in a way that readers can picture it for themselves?

You can tighten up your story by combining locations, too. Is it realistic that the *Friends* characters only went to Central Perk for coffee? Nope. But it sure is a helpful storytelling device that they did.

Characters are another place where you might be able to tighten up your story and elevate it to something iconic and memorable for readers.

- **Protagonist**
- **Love Interest** (or second protagonist[1])
- **Best Friend** (balancing force, peer on journey)
- Sibling(s) / Found **Family**
- **Mentor** (parent figure)
- **Apprentice**
- Antagonist / **Nemesis**
- **Secondary Characters** (tighten these up, make sure they're serving the story)

Just like a list of tropes and other favourite things, a list about the world you want to build and the characters you want to make sure to include can be an excellent way to **blueprint your series**.

This is a term I stole from academia when I was laid off. In my former career, part of my role was making sure that the teaching we were delivering **blueprinted** to the curriculum objectives. I would literally sit down with the two documents, our teaching plan on the left and the curriculum objectives on the right, and number them for the auditors, making sure that every element of the required curriculum was reflected in our teaching, and also, just as importantly, that we weren't spending valuable teaching time on non-curriculum stuff at the expense of the required elements.

This isn't to say that we didn't sometimes teach bonus lessons! Nothing wrong with a delightful bit of fluff. Sometimes that's the best part (and you might even add fluffy moments to a checklist! Huzzah, now fluff is a part of your blueprinting list). But you don't want to lose sight of what your goal is here. Endless tender moments aren't enough, basically.

So, at some point, I remembered this term, **blueprinting**, and when I do it, my books are tighter.

The best part is that often it's **not** about changing your core story and protagonist, but beefing up what is around them.

- Making sure your cast is hitting all the big notes (mentor/parent figure, best friend who is the opposite of the protagonist so there's delightful tension there, a love interest who complicates everything, an apprentice, a nemesis).
- Making sure the World is clear and easily accessible to readers.

Let's call this the **Netflix Test**. Could your World be turned into a TV series? If not, why not? That can be a significant difference between Series 1.0 and Series 2.0 (see Chapter Twenty-one for my thoughts on Series 2.0).

Speaking of Netflix...the other thing I've shame-lessly pinched and added to my publishing tool belt is that I think of myself as a show runner, not just a publisher. Let's dig into that in the next chapter.

---

1. Michael Hague's workshops are great for understanding the difference between a love interest and a second protagonist. I also refer you here to Gwen Hayes' excellent reference book, *Romancing the Beat*, which covers the story structure for a dual protagonist story better than anything else out there.

CHAPTER SEVENTEEN

TIPS AND TRICKS FOR "SHOW RUNNING" A SERIES

EARLIER IN THE book I talked about taking off your writing hat and putting on your marketing hat or your publisher hat. Often traditional authors talk about how daunting the prospect of wearing all those hats might be.

So let's stop thinking about them as multiple, different hats. Instead, let's compare ourselves to writers in another field. Television. Self-publishing can be like working in a writing room or being a writer-for-hire. You can pick a market and churn out works in a single brand without wearing too many different hats. Consistency is a winning strategy, for sure! So is productivity.

But people who build a brand, who become known

for a reliable type of story that readers come back for seconds on, those authors are more like show runners than a writer in a writing room or doing work-for-hire.

Show runners are doing a lot more than writing. They're doing a lot of heavy effort in pre-production, perfecting the pitch and elevating the concept to something truly fresh and hooky. They delegate work (like editing and cover design) to specialists, but the final decision—is this the right call—lies with them. They create characters and worlds that can carry the weight of a series.

Where writing genre fiction differs from show running is that we are our own writer room, unless you work with a co-writer. But even then, there are examples where show runners are heavily involved in doing the writing work, too.

So now I'll pivot away from television and back to my own work, and the lessons I've learned from "show running" ten series. Or, to be more honest, show running my most recent three series, after learning the hard way that if I didn't, the books would get away from me and the series would limp across the finish line.

CONSISTENCY AND TOOLS FOR WRITING A LONG RUNNING SERIES

- **Sketch out your first three to five books**, in the broadest of strokes, before you finish book one. This will test the series concept, and also ensure you have the books set in the best order to funnel readers down the rabbit trail. We're going to do this in the next two chapters in depth!

- **Keep track of your threads**; be it in a series bible, or Post-it notes, or by doing a reread before each new book, continue to weave the world from one book to the next. Reference back to your character checklists and make sure you bring different relationship dynamics to each book. *Don't introduce a mentor in book one and then have her disappear, only to return in book four, without mention in between.*

- Give people **more of what they love, just do it bigger and better each time.** Series get tired when they feel like stories are being retread. One way to think about this is that tropes can be the same, but plot shouldn't be, and a redo on a trope should come with a twist or a fresh take.

- Readers are looking for **emotional payoff** in fiction. They want to see glimpses of past characters they have been attached to; they want antagonists to get their due, eventually; and they really, really want you to stick the ending when you finally get there.

- Remember that map I told you to draw? Put that on a wall somewhere, or inside a binder or planner.

- Write down all pregnancies, births, deaths, injuries. Or you'll have to send an email newsletter with the subject line, "The Case of the Missing Baby[1]."

---

1. Yes, I had to do this. I forgot about a pregnancy mentioned in a single line in Pine Harbour #6, *Love in a Sandstorm*. That character, Olivia, was on the page a lot in book eight...without the baby that pregnancy may have delivered. Readers noticed immediately after the release of book eight. The emails haven't ended, and it's on my to-do list to fix. Mea culpa.

CHAPTER EIGHTEEN

SKETCHING YOUR NEXT SERIES

SO FAR, we've figured out the core of what we want our series to be, though if you're still working on that, that's okay! And you might have an idea of what book one looks like—or, you may be struggling with what book one should look like because you're worried about what the entire series will look like.

A common question I get when I talk about planning a series is how to handle the overall arc. **You don't need to know how the series will grow or end in order to start it, unless YOU need to know for yourself.** Some people plot that all out, others know turning points they'll write towards, and still others prefer to let the journey carry them wherever it will.

How do you write a series arc without knowing

where it's going? The same way we go through life, really. Your world needs to have a set of logical rules, and you need to abide by those rules, but if you have fully realized characters and you throw conflict in their path, they'll react. Then the chain reaction will commence. If you do your job as a writer, the conflict will escalate, the reactions will get bigger, and the characters will be forever changed because of the whole experience. That's true for "pantsing" a book, and it's true for a series, too.

How is writing a series different than writing a book? In book one, you make a promise to the reader —here, I give you this world. It's going to grow and get more interesting. Stay with me a while.

You want to think about **how do you feel about staying with this world?** Now is the time to fix the things that might be a barrier to writing for you in book 3, 5, 8. What can you do to make this world more interesting *for you*.

HOMEWORK #1: Imagine 3/5/8 books in this series

Balance them out in your head. Do you see the background world changing through those stories? If you're a pantser, it's okay if you don't know how it'll change, but do a gut check: **is this world dynamic enough to shift with the characters and continue to surprise and please readers?**

In the next chapter, we're going to start putting this down on paper in a really structured way, so for now, it's fine to just have them in your head.

HOMEWORK #2: figure out titles, tag lines and hooks for each of those books

THIS CAN CHANGE AGAIN. But if you are writing contemporary romance, for example, and you can't think of five different tropes you could envision happening in this world, that's a problem. If you write mystery, think about the different kinds of cases that might come up. What's the hook for each one?

For some people, this is going to be enough of a process prod. Maybe you've already sketched out the list of stories on a page, with lots of room in between them, like this:

WHISPER BEACH

Book 1 Friends Before Benefits -- Stella and Ty

.

.

.

Book 2 Married to the Enemy -- Sam and Gillian

.

.

.

Book 3 Making of a Bad Boy -- Audrey and Heath

.

.

.

Maybe you've already started to list trope-y elements under each one. Do you have a balanced series? Or do you only have the barest sketch of later books?

Or maybe you're frozen, and you need more help. Don't worry!

Turn the page for a more detailed step-by-step breakdown of how I sketched out the start to a series.

If you want to work along with me, grab your notes from earlier in the book. Your lists of tropes, characters, world elements and sketch, and maybe even the excerpt and work-to-date on book one.

Also have at hand the notes you've made on comparable series. Once you have a full series idea sketched out, you'll want to blueprint it against what you've set for yourself—both as your own vision for your brand (see chapter fifteen) but also what your most comparable similar authors have done with their projects that you admire and want to be read next to (chapter eleven).

CHAPTER NINETEEN

PLANNING OUT A SERIES OF STANDALONE ROMANCES

HERE'S how I **sketch a romance series of books with different protagonists in each book.** I took a snapshot at each point in the process where something key happened.

Again, my goal is to make sure each book is robust and balanced with respect to the essential elements compared to the others; and that I'm hitting the notes I want, especially in the **first book, and overall in the series.**

Start with a blank series worksheet. Put a space for each book you know you'll write, more space at the bottom for expanding the universe, and on the right, a column for all the various elements. I did this for three books at first, but you could do five, or even eight.

SERIES NAME:

BOOK 1:

BOOK 2:

BOOK 3:

Step 1: Jot down title ideas for the first three books, if you have them. Otherwise, leaving them as book 1/2/3 and moving on to step 2 is fine.

Step 2: Fill in the series-linked protagonists (heroes, in a band-of-brothers series, or heroines in a friendship romance saga), or if you have a single protagonist across your series, then the key trope or murder/monster of the week.

For my series, I had title ideas first, so I added those.

Series name: **Whisper Beach**

Book 1 Friends Before Benefits

Book 2 Married to the Enemy

Book 3, Making of a Bad Boy

And then I scribbled down hero names: Ty West, Sam Brodie, Heath [Doesn't Have a Last Name Yet]. I also have ideas for future heroes, so I added those names to the bottom of the page, in the big blank area.

You can add more labels now: Future Book Ideas at the bottom left, and *Must Have Elements* or Tropes to the right-hand column. I don't put them on the page at first, because I like to look at my first three ideas before expanding it wide open. But as things occur to me, I jot them down.

SERIES NAME: Whisper Beach

	TROPES: (must have elements. id list favourites)
BOOK 1: Ty West Friends Before Benefits	
BOOK 2: Sam Brodie Married to the Enemy	
BOOK 3: Heath ___ Making of a Bad Boy	
FUTURE BOOKS: Gavin Brodie Travis Brodie	

LIGHTBULB MOMENT: Some of my future heroes are brothers to one of the characters (Sam). Hmmm. That might mean Sam's book is the one that hooks most strongly to future heroes. **Maybe his book should be book 1.** (Did you have a similar lightbulb moment as you read through some of the course material? Don't be afraid to rearrange your books in a way that makes the read-through potential the most interesting for readers!)

Step 3: REARRANGE WHAT NEEDS TO BE REARRANGED!

Step 4: layer in tropes that might work.

And sure enough, when I added in my tropes, I had more ideas for book 2 (now book 1) anyway! So that reinforced my gut instinct to switch the release order.

The tropes I've added to the worksheet are:

- Friends to lovers
- Friends with benefits
- Marriage of convenience
- Enemies to lovers
- Fish out of water
- Forced proximity
- Ugly duckling
- Friends to lovers
- Unrequited love

SERIES NAME: Whisper Beach

	TROPES: (must have elements, id list favourites)
BOOK 2: Ty West **Friends Before Benefits** friends to lovers, friends with benefits	
BOOK 1: Sam Brodie **Married to the Enemy** marriage of convenience, enemies to lovers, fish out of water, forced proximity	
BOOK 3: Heath ___ **Making of a Bad Boy** friends to lovers, ugly duckling, unrequited love	
FUTURE BOOKS: Gavin Brodie Travis Brodie	

Once you've got primary protagonists and tropes, you can layer in their love interests (you may have jumped ahead and done this already!) and try to come up with a shorthand way of describing their love story. This will help you with taglines.

If you can't summarize a book in a few words, readers may struggle to do that too. It's easier to grab a few hook ideas NOW versus when the book is done and complicated and layered.

Every so often, Twitter will have a fun meme on this topic to go viral. Recently there was one that asked authors to describe their book like a Reddit r/relationships question.

My [25M] best friend [25F] is convinced I'll have a better time finding a date if I spend less time on building my business and more time on how I look. How can I tell her the only woman I want to date is the one so eager to hook me up with anyone else in our small town...but her?

That's Heath and Audrey's book in a nutshell. Or, as I shorthand it on the next page, "biz nerd + social butterfly".

SERIES NAME: Whisper Beach

	TROPES: (must have elements, id list favourites)
BOOK 2: playboy + virgin Ty West + Stella Nixon Friends Before Benefits friends to lovers, friends with benefits	
BOOK 1: grumpy + writer Sam Brodie + Gillian Ford Married to the Enemy marriage of convenience, enemies to lovers, fish out of water, forced proximity	
BOOK 3: social butterfly Heath + Audrey + biz nerd Making of a Bad Boy friends to lovers, ugly duckling, unrequited love	

FUTURE BOOKS:

Gavin Brodie

Travis Brodie

Another shorthand I like is what I call The Alisha Rai Method, because she did it on Twitter once: list the protagonists and everywhere they have sex (or, depending on your genre, run into danger, have a near miss with death, find a dead body, or have a hilarious mishap).

Then I let my mind wander—and this may take days, as I add to the list, come and go from it and think about what's missing. For this series, I have more than one friends to lovers trope, so I need to brainstorm more trope ideas for Future Books. Right now, I'm not sure what those will be, so I scrawl a very unhelpful NEED MORE HERE note to myself and move on.

I use the tropes space on the right-hand side to list scenes I definitely want to include, leaning heavily on my personal id list I developed after listening to Jennifer Lynn Barnes' workshop at RWA18 in Denver, "Writing for Your Id"[1]—everything I love about small town romances, basically, and want to see for sure in this series.

This list is longer than what I put on the example sheet that follows, and honestly, I keep this in my phone and add to it all the time. Even this list isn't complete! It's an ongoing work in progress.

Can you tell I'm a big fan of this idea?

My small town romance id list

- Fall fairs, winter carnivals
- A pier!!! Strung with lights!
- A beach bar—late night shenanigans
- Ice cream
- Wedding planner
- Town meetings
- Curmudgeon opposed to new ideas (who comes around, obviously)
- Animal adoption picnics
- Bake sales
- Hockey games
- Running into an ex at the hardware store, sweaty and mid-project

And in there are also some tropes (opposites attract, oil and water, suspicion of each other) and a specific scene I want to write (waking up together from a nap).

Step 5: Finally, I use the bottom right-hand corner to underline the themes I want to see arc over the entire series.

Step 6: fill in the rest of the page until it's overflowing with ideas (or threats to yourself if you don't come up with some good ideas).

SERIES NAME: Whisper Beach

BOOK 2: playboy + virgin
Ty West + Stella Nixon
   Friends Before Benefits
      friends to lovers,
      friends with benefits

BOOK 1: grumpy + writer
Sam Brodie + Gillian Ford
   Married to the Enemy
      marriage of convenience,
         enemies to lovers,
   fish out of water, forced proximity

BOOK 3: social butterfly
Heath + Audrey + biz nerd
   Making of a Bad Boy
      friends to lovers,
         ugly duckling,
         unrequited love

FUTURE BOOKS:

Gavin Brodie   NEED
                  MORE
Travis Brodie   HERE

TROPES:
(must have elements,
id list favourites)

wake up from
an accidental nap

opposites attract

suspicion!

oil and water

fall fair,
winter carnival

PIER
strung with lights?

Ice cream?

wedding planner?

bar on the beach
LATE NIGHT
SHENANIGANS

SERIES ARC
friendship
tourism
wineries
beach rehab
generational
tension

There is a blank copy of this complete worksheet at the back of the print copy of this book, and also on my website. If you find it useful, please let me know!

And let me leave you with three general rules to consider, if you take nothing else away from this chapter.

Rule #1: Make the first book the most universally enjoyable trope possible from your list of ideas.

Rule #2: Make the books all similar lengths. Growing in length is fine, see Harry Potter, but jerking back to a short novel after a robust full-length start is a reader disappointment waiting to happen.

Rule #3: When it comes to your *next* series after this one, make it the same, but better. (If you really feel like you must start over at some point, do it out of pure enthusiasm. And actually, that's a great metric for anything. How excited are you about this series?)

---

1. The recording of the "Writing for Your Id" workshop is available for purchase on the Romance Writers of America website. I also believe Jennifer Lynn Barnes is also releasing a book on this topic in 2020. Highly recommend you devour both!

CHAPTER TWENTY

BUT ZOE, I'M GOING TO WRITE A LONG RUNNING SERIES ABOUT A SINGLE PROTAGONIST

ONE OF THE points of feedback I got on the beta version of this book was that my step-by-step example was very romance-specific.

Yep, that's what I write. And I did try to do up an example of how I'd do the same process for a single protagonist series, but the truth is, it felt forced. Also, I'm the furthest thing from an expert in that area. Perhaps in a future edition of this book I'll have a guest chapter written by a thriller or mystery author with their perspective on that, and what their planning looks like, but I think the best advice I can offer right now is in the form of a few questions.

The answers can be scribbled down on the same blank template from the previous chapter (also in the appendix at the back of the paperback edition of this book, or available to download from my website at www.romanceyourbrand.com).

1. Is your protagonist delightfully flawed enough to learn something new about themselves in each book?
2. Do you have a list of Monster of the Week episode ideas that you can layer on top of the long-running series arc?
3. Could your first in series be turned into a movie or a Netflix series? If not, what's missing?
4. Is your cast of secondary characters diverse, robust, and archetypal?
5. Is your setting familiar enough for readers to feel at home, but also different enough to keep them turning the pages in wonder?

I mentioned that my husband writes and draws zombie stories. He always has, since long before I started writing fiction. In fact, he went to art school for illustration before taking a left turn into a career in the military. Two years ago, he got serious about wanting to write pre-apocalyptic survival horror genre fiction. (It's a mouthful!)

Why did he suddenly want to write long form fiction, after years of sketching and writing comic strip stories? Because he read one too many books that got the military details wrong.

I think many of us can relate to the feeling of wanting to write to get something correct. To nail the description or location or accents. I have a love of books set in New Zealand and Australia, for example...as long as they're written by authors *from* New Zealand and Australia. Otherwise it's painful to read, because the voice isn't authentic.

But authenticity of details does not a complete story make. This is the big learning curve my husband is currently working through, and what I went through years ago: what is the balancing point between getting it right, and making it entertaining?

At the back of this book I have a short list of recommended reads. The writing craft book I list there is *Romancing the Beat* by Gwen Hayes. For people who are writing mysteries, I have it on good authority that Sara Rosett's *How to Outline a Cozy Mystery* is an excellent resource, comparable to Gwen's book.

If you skipped the last chapter because it doesn't apply to you, I'm going to gently encourage you to go back and read it anyway. We can all learn from observing other people's processes! But just in case you zoomed right to this content, I'll paste in the three overarching rules that apply to every series architect, regardless of genre. These are copied directly from the previous chapter.

Rule #1: Make the first book the most universally enjoyable trope possible from your list of ideas.

Rule #2: Make the books all similar lengths. Growing in length is fine, see Harry Potter, but jerking back to a short novel after a robust full-length start is a reader disappointment waiting to happen.

Rule #3: When it comes to your *next* series after this one, make it the same, but better.

CHAPTER TWENTY-ONE

SERIES 2.0

A FEW YEARS AGO, I posted this on Facebook.

Random Publishing Thought #78...How to Jack Your Business to the Next Level

Spoiler alert: my answer is the same old (write more books)...but with some context.

Okay, so you've written a book, a series, and it didn't take off. Damn those magic beans. But it's good, it's got at least a couple of fans, and you know in your heart of hearts that it's something to be proud of.

What do you do?

Everyone says, write more books, right? And

deep inside, you're like, but this series is good. GOOD. I know it!

I get that. But the answer is still to write more books, and here's why: that series could be better.

So you should write Series 2.0.

Don't go veering off in another direction. Don't lose yourself deep in the bottom of a bottle of something delicious and then decide that it must be stepbrothers or bust.

Look at your series, and tweak it. Think…what would the [X number of] fans who loved Series 1.0 want to see in Series 2.0? What did I shy away from, but now I really want to do this time, because I'm a better writer? What did I sniff at because it was too commercial, and I wanted to be original, but now I really wish I was selling better?

Write whatever is at the centre of that Venn Diagram.

Meanwhile, don't give up on Series 1.0. When Series 2.0 launches, and finds new readers, some of them will funnel backwards.

But it's time to let go of the idea that if you just force Series 1.0 hard enough, it'll suddenly skyrocket to the moon. (I mean, it might. But I'd still let go of that idea because it's going to get in the way of you writing Series 2.0, and that's a much safer bet).

Writer, I cannot promise you that the first series you write after reading this book will be a hit. I can't promise you *my* next series will be a hit. That's not how publishing works.

But I can promise you that if you keep building on what you have done in the past, rather than starting over, you will see momentum.

Stick to your plan. Stick to what gets you excited, and keep building. Write Series 2.0. And then, Series 3.0.

Keep writing. Keep revising, and analyzing, and doing the hard work to suss out what resonates with readers and what doesn't motivate them to click. It's hard to look at that factor, especially if it is something we have enthusiasm for. But don't make the mistake of throwing the baby out with the bathwater. It may just need some tweaks for the same premise to work.

At the midpoint review, I recommended Robyn Carr's Virgin River series. I mentioned in an endnote on that chapter that it is also available on Netflix now as a TV series. If you watch it, or read the books, pay attention to mentions of Gold Valley.

Gold Valley was a trilogy Ms. Carr wrote for Harlequin.

Virgin River is Gold Valley 2.0. She kept writing in the same world, and went from a trilogy to a twenty-book series that is now a Netflix TV series.

Don't give up on your dreams.

CHAPTER TWENTY-TWO

IT'S THE END OF THE BOOK AS WE KNOW IT...

MY FRIEND, Gwen Hayes, had music references all the way through *Romancing the Beat*. I've only managed to sneak one in here, in the final chapter. And it's not the end of the world, just this book.

It's the end of the pre-production stage, show runners. Or maybe it's the end of the pre-pre-production stage, and you're going to loop back to the beginning! It's okay if you've fallen behind in the homework, if you've gotten overwhelmed as you move through the chapters. This is a toolbox I'm helping you build. Follow along, grab what elements are relevant to you now, and take note of what you want to try later. This is **for you**, not for me. So no feeling bad; that's counterproductive for creativity.

Hopefully by this point you have an idea for a series that sits squarely inside your genre and will appeal to a wide group of readers. **That's the point of this book: it's not a judgement on series that are more niche, or written because they make your soul happy, or more literary in nature.** But what we're focusing on here is a series that will make you some money.

Once you get that series rolling, you know what I'm going to suggest. Start planning for Series 2.0. And then it'll be time for you to **Romance Your Plan.**

———

COMING IN JUNE 2020: Romance Your Plan, book two in my Publishing How To series!

Sign up for my newsletter at www. romanceyourbrand.com to get monthly tips and news about my non-fiction books!

ZOE'S NON-FICTION HOW TO WRITE READING AND REFERENCE LIST

Romancing the Beat by Gwen Hayes

How to Outline a Cozy Mystery by Sara Rosett

The Basic Character Creation Workbook
by Tasha L. Harrison

The Science of Stories: Writing For Your Id
by Jennifer Lynn Barnes

Writer, You Need to Quit by Becca Syme

ONLINE RESOURCES

Whitney G's *Indie Tea* blog

Skye Warren's author email

Angela James's *Before You Hit Send* self-editing course

APPENDIX: WORKSHEETS

Appendix A: Your Book Here (also available at www.romanceyourbrand.com/your-book-here/)

TAP INTO YOUR ENTHUSIASM

1. Mission: Who you are, what you write, and maybe who you write it for. YOU AND YOUR GENRE.

2. Vision: WHAT YOU LOVE. Your favourite tropes, sub-genres, archetypes, and story structures.

3. Action Plan: Put THAT ON THE PAGE. Nothing else. Harness your enthusiasm and write exactly what you want to write, in the form that is most compatible with commercial fiction.

THAT ON THE PAGE

WHAT YOU LOVE

YOU & YOUR GENRE

ROMANCE YOUR BRAND
MISSION / VISION / ACTION PLAN

Appendix B: Tap Into Your Enthusiasm (also available at www.romanceyourbrand.com/mission-vision-action-plan/)

MEDIA KIT FOR [TITLE]

LOGLINE

Series:
Author(s):

BUY LINKS (full):

Apple:
Nook:
Kobo:
Google:
Amazon US:
Amazon UK:
Amazon AU:
Amazon CA:
Amazon DE:

BUY LINKS (shortened):

Apple:
Nook:
Kobo:
Amazon*:
Google:

* some people use a redirect link for all the Amazon stores so you only need one link here
instead of all of them

BLURB:

SHORT BLURB:

EXCERPT #1:

EXCERPT #2:

EXCERPT #3:

TROPE LIST:

THIS MEETS THAT COMPARISON:

Appendix C: Media Kit template (also available at
www.romanceyourbrand.com/media-kit-template/)

SERIES NAME:

BOOK 1:	TROPES: (must have elements, id list favourites)
BOOK 2:	
BOOK 3:	
FUTURE BOOKS:	**RULE #1** BOOK 1: most universal trope/ character archetype **RULE #2** ALL BOOKS: similar length **RULE #3:** NEXT SERIES: Build on your previous success OR start again with bold excitement

Appendix D: Sketching a Series Worksheet (also available
at www.romanceyourbrand.com/planning-a-series/)

CPSIA information can be obtained
at www.ICGtesting.com
Printed in the USA
LVHW040731301219
642041LV00006B/1161/P

9 781989 703236